LET IT ROT!

To Gregory

*May he, like his father, have
the chance to pursue what interests
him most.*

LET IT

The Gardener's

A Garden Way Publishing Book

 Storey Communications, Inc.
Pownal, Vermont 05261

ROT!

Guide to **Composting**

by Stu Campbell

Contents

"One aker well compast, is worth akers three . . ."
—*Tusser (1557)*

"Now I am terrified at the Earth, it is that calm and patient,
It grows such sweet things out of such corruptions,
It turns harmless and stainless on its axis, with such
endless succession of diseased corpses,
It distills exquisite winds out of such infused fetor,
It gives such divine materials to men, and accepts such
leavings from them at last."

—*Walt Whitman, "This Compost"*

Introduction

W ERE you watching television during Christmas week, 1968? That's a tough question. You probably can't recall. It's in the nature of much television to be immemorable.

But if you had your set on at all that week, you will surely remember a series of live broadcasts that was beamed to earth from outer space. On Christmas Eve that year the astronaut crew of the Apollo 8 space mission, Frank Borman, Jim Lovell and Bill Anders, were inspired — from a location near the moon — to read to us from the first chapter of *Genesis*.

> In the beginning God created the heaven and the earth. And the earth was without form, and void; and the darkness was upon the face of the deep. And the Spirit of God moved upon the face of the waters . . .
> And God said, Let there be light: and there was light . . .

Never before could these words have held such profound meaning for earth's inhabitants. The context in which they were uttered was unique in man's collective experience. Three men had travelled far beyond a point where men had ever ventured, and though some of their successors on later missions were to see more than they, and accomplish still greater feats, the crew of Apollo 8 was viewing earth from a totally fresh — *cosmic* — perspective.

In the dark and lifeless void of space the astronauts were understandably lonely, and happy to be on their way home. But as they looked at us from tens of thousands of miles away, they must have felt somehow divorced from us too. It was almost as if man was having his first glimpse at himself and at his planet as an outsider might see us. These three were being afforded incalcuable insight.

"What I keep imagining," said Jim Lovell, "is if I were some lonely traveler from another planet, what I would think about the earth, whether I think it would be inhabited or not."

All three members of the crew were struck by the vulnerable-looking tininess of their mother planet.

Borman commented, "We are one hunk of ground, water, air floating around in space. From out there it is really one world . . . The view of earth from the moon fascinated me — a small disk 240,000 miles away. It is hard to think that that little thing held so many problems, so many frustrations. Raging nationalistic interests, famines, and pestilence don't show from that distance. I'm convinced that some wayward stranger and spacecraft would certainly know instinctively that if earth were inhabited, then the destinies of all who lived on it must inevitably be interwoven and joined."

Major Borman's strong feelings about the common destiny of all men were hardly new. They had been expressed countless times before by poets, philosophers, clergymen, even politicians. What was *new* was the vision that inspired him — a vision that no photograph taken from a satellite or any artist's rendition could duplicate. In many ways this earthview marked a new starting point in human history.

The reality of earth's limited nature was brought home to them with startling clarity. During the first part of their voyage they had concentrated almost solely on the moon, with hardly a homeward glance. But now they had been through the breath-holding ordeal of passing around and behind it, and could see the earth suspended before them outside the window of the spacecraft. They suddenly recognized it for what it was and is — a completely closed system, a planet with an ever dwindling supply of nonrenewable resources and a too-abundant supply of people. They were jolted into an awareness that, for the time being at least, there can probably be no help — other than spiritual sustenance — from anywhere else in the universe.

"Up there it's a black and white world." said Lovell. "There is no color. In the whole universe, wherever we looked, the only bit of color was back on earth. There we could see the royal blue of the seas, the tans and browns of the land, and the white of the clouds. It was just another body, really, about four times bigger than the moon. But it held all the hope and all the life and all the things that the crew of Apollo knew and loved. It was the most beautiful thing there was in all the heavens. People down there don't realize what they have, maybe because not many of them have the opportunity to leave it, and then come back again as we did."

The profundity of the Apollo 8 telecasts has worn off by now. The frightening "energy crisis" of the winter of 1974, — either real or fabricated — has been held at bay. We are told that we can relax and breathe a bit, and are reminded that necessity is the mother of invention. Technology will find all the right answers we are told. Humanity's capacity for ingenuity and inventiveness is boundless. Maybe we *shouldn't* worry so much.

Proponents of our N.A.S.A. program and certain space experts such as German-born Krafft Ehricke, interviewed recently in *Intellectual Digest,* see the many pessimistic environmentalists, nutritionists, economists and energy experts who forecast further and far more severe shortages of raw materials, clean air, fresh water, fertilizers, fossil fuels, arable land and food, as defeatists who have already stuck their heads in the sand to await their doom.

They are right in saying that we should be taking a more positive approach than some of us seem to be taking. They also maintain that we should not accept any sort of planned economic regression. We should be working to *expand* our vision, and not be sitting gloomily back waiting for our terrestrial environment to shrink as we gradually poison ourselves and use up what resources we have left.

They object to the metaphor of earth as a spaceship drifting helplessly in a hostile medium of infinite dimensions. We should try to see ourselves instead, they say, as passengers on a cruise ship surrounded by friendly freighters. We should be trying to enlarge our resource base, they tell us, by exploiting the raw materials of some of those other worlds that are nearest to us.

Humans have not yet reached the zenith of their development, they claim. They are just at the beginning of their growth. Humanity is like a fetus in its eighth month. Sitting inside our little womb, we are troubled by the debris which floats by and are starting to realize that quarters are getting pretty close. The tenth and eleventh months look dismal indeed. Must we conclude from all of this empirical evidence that we should stop growing altogether? With enough foresight we might see that, figuratively speaking, in another month or so a whole new universe will open up to us.

The same people suggest that we can continue to forge ahead at an economic pace equal to the one we have established for ourselves. Damn the consequences! We can find answers and solutions later, and they have faith that we will. We can solve our pollution problems, for instance, by slinging our municipal, industrial and even radioactive wastes far into deep space where we can forget about them forever.

Ehricke, who obviously loves his planet as much as the next man, points out that an earth without waste products and fed from sources outside itself, could become the "garden of the solar system." He suggests that the rest of the solar system might be useful in ways we have not even begun to comprehend, and that by refusing to allow ourselves to find out more, we are, in effect, rolling over and playing dead.

There is a great deal of psychological wisdom in what they have to say. We cannot allow ourselves to become helpless and despondent pessimists, nor can we afford to adopt an eat-drink-and-be-merry philosophy. The rest of the universe *may* hold great promise for us.

But to operate at this point under the assumption that man's rebirth is imminent and that we can permit ourselves to expend all of what we have, trusting that soon resources from outer space will be readily available, is to seriously believe in science fiction. We are a long way from being capable of mining on the moon or growing food on Mars.

The truth is that "this old house" we live in is going to have to do us quite a bit longer. We are in no position either to move or to do any sort of major remodeling job to make it more the garden spot of the universe. All of the necessary raw materials are no longer — or are not yet — available.

It is not yet time to jettison potentially valuable stuff out the window of our biosphere. Humans are not even close — emotionally, politically, physically, spiritually or even technologically — to being true citizens of the cosmos as a whole.

The time *has* come, like it or not, to *further* encourage and promote the simple arts of conservation, recycling, thoughtful food cultivation and storage. We had *better* learn to live frugally, while the scientists and intellectuals explore the resource possibilities outside of our world. In the meantime, we should be looking for smaller and less complicated social and industrial mechanisms for developing humanistic "intermediate technology" which can help us feed ourselves, create interesting, dignified, and useful work for lots of people and save energy at the same time.

We are going to *have* to "wind down" for a while. We may have to postpone and shrink the scope of our physical goals to stay in keeping with the restricting limitations imposed by our fragile environment. Our spirit need not weaken for a second in its willingness to investigate every conceivable horizon, but the flesh may have to learn to live with a set of different — and perhaps less luxurious — circumstances.

Flush times may be over. We might be smart to start looking behind us as well as ahead. There is much to be found there, too. Ancient man seemed to have an innate sensitivity not only to his own needs, but to those of his soil, his domestic creatures, his growing things. He knew the value of recycling and making the best of what he had. But somehow, somewhere along the line, this sensitivity has become atrophied in much of modern man. While modern chemists seek ways to transform inorganic matter into food, let's try to do the best we can with old methods — by protecting and using our soil properly.

In some "backwater" corners of the earth the old ideas of using things up, wearing things out, making things do, or doing without, have changed very little over the centuries. Do you know that it is hard to communicate the idea of "waste" to a non-English speaking Chinese? He simply won't understand what you are talking about. To him the bad by-products of something are potentially good materials for something else. Perhaps we should be looking more to our agricultural ancestors, and should turn for counsel to some of those who we have long felt were the "underdeveloped" members of the earth's community. They can teach us much about a less consumptive lifestyle.

It is high time we reversed some trends. Cancerous cities everywhere have in large measure outlived their usefulness. Urban populations generally need to be reduced, and people need to be spread around more evenly — dispersed and decentralized. Isn't there some way we can stop paving over places that could be used for growing food? Couldn't we somehow dismantle parts of our cities, reuse some of the old building materials, and let some of the concrete go to seed?

Waste can simply no longer be tolerated. The time is long past when we can afford to throw so many things away, either into the outer galaxies or here on earth. It's time for all of us to discover the larger benefits and cosmic beauty of little earthly things like composting.

Genesis, in the King James version, continues:

> .... God said, Let the earth bring forth grass, the herb yielding seed, and the fruit tree yielding fruit after its kind, whose seed is in itself, upon the earth: and it was so. And the earth brought forth grass, and herb yielding seed after his kind, and the tree yielding fruit whose seed was itself after his kind: and God saw that it was good.

It is *still* good. It is good for *us* in terms of what we know — though this should be no excuse for not knowing more. And *for* all we know right now, this God-wrought and man-defiled place may already be the garden of the universe — with all of its imperfections. We must preserve and nurture it as best we can, for ourselves and for our children.

1

Home Composting: Art or Science

S OMEWHERE, thousands and thousands of years ago, some hairy and slouched man-creature who groveled in the dirt with his hands or with a stick and who managed to grow himself some food, may have discovered that seeds grew better near the place where his woman-creature piled the apparently useless refuse from their cave or hut. Most of this "waste" material was organic matter.

I doubt very much that at the moment of discovery he had either the wisdom or the inclination to shout "Eureka!" But he — or his son, or his son's son — must have told his friends about it, because the idea of putting human, animal, vegetable and mineral wastes on or into the soil to make it better spread to all corners of the world.

In the beginning there was manure. You might recall that the Biblical figure Job, poor fellow, was occasionally left sitting on a dung heap while God and Satan argued about the state of his soul. Man has known for a long time that animal excrement is valuable stuff when it comes to growing things, and he has apparently always made efforts to save it. But shortly after he became friendly enough with animals to be able to persuade a few of them to live at home with him in a more or less peaceful relationship, he must have realized that there was never quite enough manure to go around. So he began to devise ways of stretching it, and started to think about ways to make "synthetic manure." He didn't know what he was doing, really. He probably just took a look at what was going on around him, and then began trying things. Composting did not begin with him.

Decomposition is at least as old as the soil. The earth itself, as the poet Walt Whitman suggests, is something of a compost pile. "It gives such divine materials to men, and accepts such leavings from them at last." Long before there were men around to observe it, composting was going on in every forest, every meadow, every swamp, and bog, and prairie and steppe in the world. As Richard Langer says, "Composting is a natural process that began with the first plants on earth and has been going on ever since."

Ancient man was the real father of organic gardening — in spite of whatever valid claims people like Sir Albert Howard or Rudolf Steiner or J. I. Rodale may have to the *modern* title. Whoever and wherever he was, he was an artist, not a scientist. Only by trial and error was he able to learn what worked when it came to making synthetic manure. He didn't have anyone to guide him or to give him good advice because there was nobody around who knew very much. Things like psychrophylic bacteria and the relationship between carbon and nitrogen in the process of decomposition were the furthest things from his mind — and at least thirty centuries away in terms of time.

All he saw, maybe, was the forest floor where leaves fell, turned dark, and gradually disappeared to be transformed into the dark, fertile soil gardeners were someday to call "humus". He must have realized that in time many things *rot* whether we try to do anything about it or not. Leave everything to Mother Nature and eventually the conditions which encourage decay will establish themselves. We can be thankful that this is something that has been going on since shortly after the beginning of time.

But allowing nature to take its course may take more time than *you* have. *The modern practice of composting is little more than speeding up and intensifying natural processes.* That's *all* it is. When you come right down to it, finished compost is no more than "treated" or "predigested" — rotted — organic matter which usually has undergone a natural heating process and which is very valuable stuff to incorporate into your garden's soil. No amount of mysterious mumbo-jumbo or scientific jargon can make it otherwise.

For too long there has been an air of cultish mysticism surrounding the art of composting. This is the kind of nonsense so many people find objectionable in a lot of composting literature. It is easy to get confused by certain gardening magazines and gardening books which discuss either a wide range of unusual composting habits and styles, or describe the "science" of composting in such narrowly-defined terms that you get the distinct impression that there is one, and *only* one method for making humus.

Don't misunderstand: there has been all kinds of *extremely* valuable scientific research done on composting, and much of the information gathered can be very helpful to the home composter as well as to the municipality that is doing or considering composting on a large scale. I suggest that you try to learn as much about the highly technical aspects of the subject as you can. But I caution that an overly-scientific approach to composting may take all the fun out of it.

To be a successful composter takes several things:

1) the realization that no matter what you do, no matter how many little mistakes you make, (a big mistake might be trying to activate your pile with something like gasoline), you are still probably going to come up with reasonably good, usable compost.

2) a basic understanding of the life forms and processes which

operate within a compost pile.

   3) a willingness to experiment.

   4) a little effort.

   5) a little artistry.

The word "compost" comes from two Latin roots, one meaning "together", the other meaning "to bring". To make edible "fruit compost" (or "fruit compote") for example, is to bring together several different kinds of fruit (in New England, at least, this can be whatever fruit you have on hand), mix them with sugar and other ingredients in a jar or crock, and let it sit to ferment for several days. It really doesn't matter how long it sits or precisely how much you add of what. In fact, you might eat some of the mixture, and when the container gets low, replenish it with other fixings as they become available. The final concoction is almost always a delicious one, though rarely, if ever, the same as the last. There are really as many recipes for making fruit compost as there are fruit compote makers — probably more.

As you get into composting try not to get bogged down with complicated recipes and formulas. A few simple guidelines can help you eliminate some of the traditionally unpleasant aspects of composting. There are very few hard-and-fast rules governing the making of good compost which must be followed to the letter.

If you are a beginner, start thinking in simple terms about a compost system. Later, you may want to develop more complicated and sophisticated techniques. Apply what scientific knowledge you have. If you find a particular section of the book too technical, skip it. You can always return to it at a later point.

Be creative. Select what you can from the information offered here and go on to establish your own composting style. When your neighbor tells you that you are doing it "all wrong", tell him that he's full of baloney. As you learn more and more about composting and begin to understand the rotting process a little better, you may grow to appreciate the recycling activity that takes place in nature day in and day out. You may also find, as others have, that you want to synchronize yourself with it.

Composting is based on the "principal of return", a principal by which all good organic gardeners try to live. But you don't have to be a purely organic gardener to be a composter. I have become more aware, sometimes with the help of organic gardening friends, that all of life is part of a continuous pattern which should not be interrupted. As men we reap things from the land in the form of produce. But this is only one small part of a much larger picture. There are many other life forms besides ourselves that come into play and help to make the cycle run. Giving *back* to the land is every bit as vital as taking *from* it. And we have taken too much for too long. Although we may never be able to offset the damage we have done to the soil and replace *all* that we have taken from it, it is not too late to try to make amends. Composting is a way of *using up* what we have in abundance — humble things like weeds, and dead grass, and garbage and old sticks — to repay a long-standing debt to the earth. By becoming more and more attuned to the mechanics of Mother Nature you realize that, as my friend Catherine Foster says in her book, *The Organic Gardener,* "In the process of nature there is no throwing away."

My wife has often gently accused me of being a tightwad and a packrat. She is probably right. I find it more and more difficult to throw *anything* out — particularly anything that had its origin in some living thing and is potential compost material. Rather than argue with me, she has learned to throw out *really* worthless things when I'm not around, in the hope that I won't notice. I have told her over and over again that she should have realized when she decided to marry someone with a name like Stuart Duncan Campbell, that that person would probably turn out to be something of a thrifty soul. My Scottish heritage seems to make me a more natural composter than she, but she is gradually coming around to my way of thinking.

Serious composters tend to reach a point where they view most of the solid and liquid material in the world as falling into one of three categories: 1) desirable compostable stuff, 2) undesirable compostable stuff, and 3) non-biodegradable stuff. I sometimes have to resist the urge to stop by the side of the road and gather up a particularly attractive bunch of leaves or cut weeds. While watching television a few evenings ago, I couldn't help but notice the beautiful clumps of kelp two lovers kept treading on as they walked arm in arm along a California beach in some low-budget film. I found myself wondering if maybe our garden couldn't use a little boron and perhaps a touch of the iodine contained in seaweed. I then started wishing that I could have some of that kelp for my compost pile. I soon lost the thread of the plot and decided to go to bed. This kind of thing doesn't happen *all* the time, mind you.

The basic thread here is this: Let common sense and the organic materials which are most available to you be your number one and number two composting guides. After that, I hope *Let It Rot!* will be of some help.

2

What You Can't See Helps You

As a nation we seem to worship cleanliness — at least it would appear that way to anyone watching television for an hour. But at times, we seem helpless to solve the problems of the massive pollution we have brought upon ourselves. Many of us live in squeamish horror of "germs" and "bugs," of "odor-causing bacteria," "wormy things," "rot" and the "fungus among us." So we spray our outdoors with insecticides and our indoors with disinfectants. We use Lysol and Bactine and Ban. We develop anti-rot paints and nonbiodegradable plastics. Maybe the time has come for us to start being less compulsive about worms, insects and bacteria and become more conscious of how these things benefit us rather than harm us. Things might be better if we *let them rot!*

Let's begin by talking about composting's lowest common denominators: the organisms which make the miracle of decomposition possible. To do this means that we have to discuss some of the most technical aspects of composting first. But they are not as complicated as you might think. If you can become familiar enough with some of the terms mentioned here, so that you can recognize them later in the book, you will be able to better understand why certain recommended composting practices should be followed.

One day I asked a friend of mine, who holds a Ph.D. in microbiology — he's a good gardener too — to sit down with me and explain a few things about fungus and bacteria. I wanted him to tell

21

me what *really* goes on under all those chopped leaves and hay in my compost pile. I couldn't understand all of what he said, but I learned this much:

MICROORGANISMS

Sir Albert Howard, the British organic horticulturalist who did much to remind modern man of the value of composting, tells us that it is living microorganisms too small for man to see, *not* human beings which are the agents that make compost. We'd be in big trouble if all microbial activity were to suddenly stop. Think of all the millions of tons of organic refuse produced in the world each day — the leaves, the grass clippings, the garbage, the industrial waste, everything. Without tiny microorganisms to digest this refuse, not only would most of it stay around, but almost ninety-nine percent of all the carbon dioxide — which you and I exhale for the most part — produced in the world, would *not* be produced. That doesn't seem so bad — we use only oxygen after all — until we realize that without carbon dioxide no plants would grow.

In other words, without microorganisms there would be no decomposition, and the vital elements which are tied up in organic materials would never get released. All organic raw material, either left to rot on its own or put into man-made compost systems, is in a crude form and contains substances which permit plants to grow. It is in a state which makes these substances *unavailable* to them. We need bacteria and fungi to do their work so that the nutrients locked up in vegetable and animal matter can be released. By continually digesting *organics,* microorganisms keep a constant flow of *in*organic nutrients going to plants. In this sense they are microscopic refineries, alchemists, and garbage men all rolled into one.

MACROORGANISMS

Not all decomposition is microbiological. Just so you don't get the wrong impression, some mention should be made of the microorganisms' much larger helpers called quite naturally, macroorganisms. Macroorganisms — creatures you *can* see — include earthworms, mites, grubs, insects and nematodes. They dig, chew, digest and mix compostable materials. Insects, of course, eat organic matter and increase the surface area for the bacteria and fungi to get at by chewing it into smaller pieces. Their excrement is also digested by the bacteria, causing more nutrients to be released.

Although they will be discussed in detail in Chapter 8, any discussion of decomposition would be impossible without mentioning the earthworm. Earthworms also ingest and *dig*est organic matter. But they can be found where they are, not only because organic matter is there, but because they seem to have a cooperative, *symbiotic,* relationship with bacteria. They do a lot of digesting for the bacteria. The bacteria do a lot of digesting for them, and provide food themselves. As earthworms eat decaying matter they also take in and metabolize many of these microorganisms. My microbiologist friend says, "A worm is like a cow grazing on a field of bacteria. A bacteria is an unbelieveably nutritious organism . . . fatless . . . sixty percent protein." The presence of earthworms in either compost or soil is evidence of good microbial activity.

An earthworm eating its way through a compost pile, passes organic matter through his body, grinding it with the help of tiny stones in his gizzard, and leaves dark, fertile, granular "castings" behind him. A worm can produce his weight in castings each day.

These granules are rich in plant nutrients which might otherwise be unavailable to plants. What happens is that worms digest microorganisms and organic debris and excrete what they do not need for their own nutrition in their casts. Together with the microorganisms they are continually liberating important chemicals into the compost or into the soil. It might not be too much of an oversimplification to say that an earthworm helps "predigest" compost for plants. Even when macroorganisms die and decay, their decomposing bodies add nitrogen and other elements to the compost, as do the minuscule bodies of bacteria.

BACTERIA AND HOW THEY GROW

There are literally thousands and thousands of different kinds of bacteria and fungi. It is ridiculous to try to learn about *all* the different microorganisms that are at work in your compost. Compost scientists suggest that it is practically impossible even to *identify* all the creatures in a single compost pile. There is only one thing we can be sure about. The more "mixed" the population of microorganisms, the better. Each type of bacteria is suited to a very specific environment. When the conditions in their surroundings change, even a little, the character of the bacterial population changes. But this is nothing *you* need to worry about. The microorganisms will automatically make their own adjustments in population. All you have to do is keep them well aired, well supplied with moisture, and well fed.

To grow and multiply, microorganisms need at least three things — besides oxygen and moisture which all compost piles should have:

(1) an *energy source,* which usually can be found in the form of a carbon compound. This might be a simple sugar which is the product of photosynthesis in any green plant; it might be *cellulose* (the stuff that plant cell walls are made of); or it might be *lignin* (one of the chief constituents of wood fiber).

(2) a *nitrogen source* normally found in the protein of the various natural activators which will be recommended in Chapter 5. If a compost pile *lacks* nitrogen, it probably has a low bacteria count. This means that carbon — in the form of straw for example — cannot be digested quickly and changed into humus.

(3) a *vitamin source.* Sufficient vitamins can be found in most plant and animal tissue, in spite of what advertisements for human vitamin supplements say. So you don't need to worry about that either.

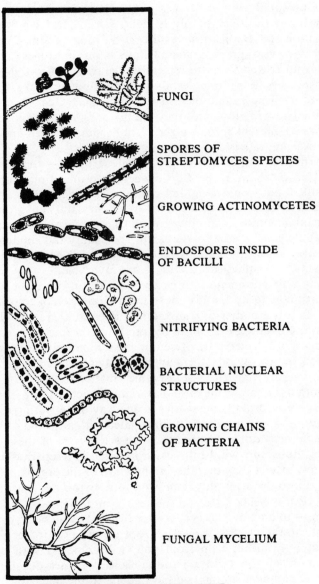

FUNGI

SPORES OF
STREPTOMYCES SPECIES

GROWING ACTINOMYCETES

ENDOSPORES INSIDE
OF BACILLI

NITRIFYING BACTERIA

BACTERIAL NUCLEAR
STRUCTURES

GROWING CHAINS
OF BACTERIA

FUNGAL MYCELIUM

A FEW TYPES OF MICROORGANISMS THAT
MIGHT APPEAR IN A COMPOST PILE.

The potential for growth in a population of microorganisms is staggering if the food supply is right. Given ideal conditions, a population of bacteria known as *Escherichia coli,* for example — we each have several grams of these fellows in our intestines (although there is no reason to try to remember the name) — will double in numbers every twenty minutes. Bacteria multiply by means of *binary fission,* which means that they literally split apart. One cell splits into two, the two will grow until they are mature and then divide again into four. Four will become eight, eight becomes sixteen and so on. Each cycle repeats itself every twenty minutes.

This means — in the believe-it-or-not department — that one gram of *"E." coli* (about 1/28 of an ounce) given an infinite supply of available food, would weigh an ounce at the end of two hours, a pound in three hours, and a ton in seven hours. If it kept growing at this maximum rate for another day and a half, it would form a mass that would equal the size of the earth. The quality and abundance of available nutrients is the only factor which limits bacterial production when other physical conditions are favorable.

Many neophyte composters worry about getting the right bacteria into their compost piles. It's not so much a question of getting them there, as it is a matter of realizing that they are there already. Dr. Clarence Goulueke, one of this country's foremost experts on composting says, "Bacteria are present in great numbers on all exposed objects." In other words, there are millions of different bacteria and fungi in any handful of organic matter. Many of these microorganisms are in the form of dormant, inactive *spores*. Feeding these spores more organic matter is one way of activating them.

Compost does not need to be inoculated with any kind of special "bacterial activator" — although there are several of these on the market. Activators will be discussed in detail in a separate section. For now, just let's say that the combination of the organic material you put into the heap plus some kind of easy-to-find "natural" activator will provide all of the necessary ingredients to get things stewing — microbiologically speaking. In twenty-four hours or so the laws of natural selection will take care of everything. Mother Nature, without any further help from you, will come up with a large population of the right microorganisms to start decomposing whatever organic material you have added to the pile.

AEROBES VERSUS ANAEROBES

Some compost piles do not "breathe." This means that gases do not pass in and out of the pile as readily as they should. Not enough oxygen can go in and not enough carbon dioxide can escape. When this happens *aerobic bacteria,* which live only where there is an available supply of oxygen, are replaced by *anaerobes* — nonoxygen consuming bacteria. Once this is the case the decomposition rate can slow by as much as ninety percent.

An aerobe needs oxygen if he is to do his work and survive. In most cases, he does better work than the anaerobe because he can do a *complete* job of composting. The anaerobe, for all his efforts, cannot. As the aerobe and his cohorts break down simple sugars into carbon dioxide and water (things that are immediately available to plants), they are also producing a lot of energy. This gives them a distinct advantage, because they can use this energy to grow that much faster themselves, and decompose that much more material. At the same time, and no less important, they excrete plant nutrients such as phosphorous, nitrogen and magnesium, to name just a few.

Meanwhile, back at the airtight heap, the anaerobe struggles to produce carbon dioxide, water, energy and nutrients too — although in much smaller quantities when compared to the aerobe's performance. The anaerobe can never digest organic matter as completely as can his oxygen-using counterpart. Along with the good things he manages to put out, he also produces a lot of useless organic acids and amines (ammonia-like substances) which are smelly, contain unavailable nitrogen, and, in some cases, are toxic to plants. Some of the end products of the anaerobe's efforts are *hydrogen sulfide* (which smells exactly like rotten eggs), *cadaverine, spermine,* and *putrescine.* These last three descriptive names do a great deal to explain the nauseating odor of an anaerobic compost pile. These are just a few reasons why this book will seem to place so much emphasis on keeping the pile well aerated.

PSYCHROPHILES, MESOPHILES AND THERMOPHILES

How does the process of bacterial decomposition work? The first wave of microbial invasion into a compost pile may be by cool-temperature aerobic bacteria called *psychrophiles.* Psychrophiles do their best work at around 55 degrees Fahrenheit, not far above refrigeration temperature. They attack the organic matter and start releasing nutrients in the form of amino acids.

When these microbes start digesting carbon compounds, the carbon is literally burned or *oxidized,* to use a more exact term. Part of this oxidative energy is given off in the form of heat. In fact, heat is the by-product of any bacterial metabolism, but contrary to what many people believe, it plays no part in the actual breaking down of organic matter. A rise in temperature, either as a result of intense bacterial activity inside the pile, or as the result of higher atmospheric temperature outside the pile will introduce different strains of organisms which grow most efficiently in this warmer climate. Remember that any change in temperature, moisture content or a dozen other conditions usually means that different microbes are going to show up. The second invasion, then, would be by a general category of bacteria called *mesophiles.*

Most of the decomposition that takes place in a compost pile is mesophilic. Some microbiologists have gone so far as to say that mesophiles are as efficient — even *more* efficient — than their higher-temperature cousins, the bacteria usually associated with successful composting. This means that if your pile does not get *extremely* hot — heat being something which most composters like to achieve — decomposition is still taking place at a pretty good rate. The only problem posed by a failure to reach a high temperature is that disease-causing organisms and weed seeds are not so easily killed at mesophilic temperatures.

Mesophiles are comfortable at about the same temperature you and I are — around 70 to 90 degrees Fahrenheit. As a matter of fact, if you were to start a compost pile in July when the temperature was consistently within this range, mesophiles would take over right away and the psychrophilic process would be eliminated altogether.

But don't be misled. A compost pile can be started any time. Fall is the time when most materials are most available to the average gardener. The period from the middle of November to about the middle of April, here in Vermont at least, is the time of least microbial activity. But there is still *some* action. Because psychrophiles operate at such low temperatures — they are still quite effective at 28 degrees Fahrenheit — decomposition takes place even in wintertime. Psychrophiles are very tenacious. Ice cream in a deep freeze will show a gradual increase in bacterial population, even though it may be months before the population will actually double.

If mesophiles generate too much heat they usually self-destruct. They get so wrapped up in their work and show such an intense rate of activity that they increase the temperature of their surroundings, and work themselves right out of a compatible environment. The usually accepted line of demarcation between mesophilic and thermophilic activity is 104 degrees. *Thermophiles,* bacteria that do their thing in heat up to and above 160 degrees Farenheit, then take over. They will raise the temperature of the pile again until hopefully, it stabilizes at somewhere near 158 degrees.

Some compost makers expect the pile to remain at this temperature peak for a sustained period of time and are disappointed when it returns to somewhere near the normal atmospheric temperature. In most cases, unless a pile is constantly fed new materials, carefully monitored and turned at strategic times, the highest-range temperatures will last from three to five days only. But this is long enough for the thermophiles to perform their function. A gradual drop in temperature is not *necessarily* a sign that the compost is complete, nor an indication that the pile has become inactive as some believe, but merely shows that the thermophiles have completed *their* work. It is now time for the mesophiles to come back into play.

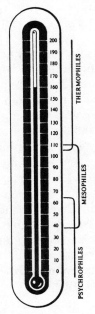

Any one of these three types of microorganisms will continue metabolizing organic matter either until they are replaced by some other microbe or until there is nothing left to consume. At that point, they might die from lack of oxygen (and anaerobes would start to do *their* thing), or they might become inactive or die because there is no more carbon or nitrogen. Whenever bacteria die off in large numbers or take on the form of inactive spores, it is usually because all the available nutrients have been released, and bacterial decomposition, for the most part, is complete.

FUNGI AND ACTINOMYCETES

While bacteria enact their changing of the guard and go about performing their various transformations of materials, there are other forms of life at work. Cool-temperature fungi, for instance, start breaking down tough cellulose and lignin along with the psychrophilic bacteria. Thermophilic fungi usually appear in the pile four to six days after the pile has been constructed.

Actinomycetes have been described as a sort of "half-breed organism" — part bacteria, part fungus that operate at medium temperatures or in the moderate heat zones of the pile. When the pile is very hot near its core they, like earthworms and mesophilic fungi, will work around the outer fringes. In large clusters, they are easy to spot and become most evident during the later stages of decomposition.

As you look inside your pile, you may notice a "grayish cobwebby" look among some of the fibrous material there. This is actinomycetes and it ought not to be confused with the pale green mold which is a sign of an oxygenless condition in a compost heap. Actinomycetes gives nearly finished compost a pleasing earthy smell. Anaerobic mold has a very different and distinct odor which, I assure you, you will recognize immediately as anything but pleasant.

In many ways the fungi and actinomycetes do the dirty work, cleaning up after the bacteria, consuming what they leave behind. They decompose the very toughest things: the remaining cellulose, starches, proteins, and lignin. Given a chance, they will even rot paper which, because it is made largely of lignin, is very difficult to break down. If you are good at remembering names, two of the most common and beneficial kinds of actinomycetes are *Streptomycetes* and *Micromonospora*. Drop those names to the neighbor who thinks you know nothing about composting.

ENZYMES

Enzymes are substances which bacteria produce. Their actual role in decomposition is a source of minor debate among microbiologists. But one thing about them is clear. They remain in the compost long after their parent bacteria have died off. While the bacteria are alive, the enzymes apparently assist in breaking down complex carbohydrates into simpler forms which the bacteria can use as food. For instance, *cellulase enzymes* attack cellulose, which in most vegetable materials is very resistant to rot. These enzymes help the fungi and actinomycetes that are trying to accomplish the same thing. What is most interesting is that they *continue* working away at the cellulose and lignin long after the microorganisms that produced them have died and become just another part of the compost.

PATHOGENS

The preoccupation that many composters have with *pathogenic organisms* — disease-causing microbes — is, in some ways, silly. They, like other bacteria, are everywhere. Just because a particular disease is a rare one, this does not mean that the organism which causes it is hard to find. The trick is not to add to their numbers. Obviously, it would be foolish to grind up a lot of clearly diseased plants and use them directly on the garden as mulch. But you *might* use them in your compost pile.

If the pile is active, pathogens will not have a chance there. Fortunately, when pathogens have to compete with nonpathogens for food, they will normally lose. Once beneficial bacteria get the upper hand, they will probably do two things: (1) They will eventually raise the temperature of the pile. Almost no pathogenic organisms can survive in temperatures much above 140 degrees Farenheit. Allowing temperatures to rise this much for sanitary reasons is called "thermal kill" or "partial sterilization." (2) The beneficial bacteria will start producing organic compounds which actually inhibit the growth of disease-causing bacteria. You and I know *these* compounds as "antibiotics." Finished compost, in almost all cases where the pile has been carefully planned and properly maintained, is virtually disease free.

THE MICROCOMMUNITY

As you can see, there is little in the rotting process to be squeamish about. Like anything else, once you understand a little about it, it makes good sense and becomes less of a disgusting mystery. In building a compost pile, you are doing a great deal more than making something useful out of something apparently worthless, although that alone is gratifying enough.

You are also creating a microcosm, a miniworld, a microcommunity, the population and character of which will be constantly changing and self-adjusting. You are initiating a series of events and conditions over which shortly you will have only minimal control. This can be a awesome thought if you have no knowledge of the governing system of checks and balances which nature — not you — establishes within the pile.

Once the micro and macrobiological machinery is set in motion, all you can do is sit back and observe, intervening only when major things like the oxygen content and moisture content of the pile need some attention. If you feel somewhat god-like, as you first create your little universe in your backyard, your growing astonishment at the scope and speed of what is happening, will replace whatever feelings of power you may have with real humility.

In comparison to man, microorganisms are Titans if allowed to exist in any kind of favorable environment. The more you understand about what they do and what they need, the more you can help them. Our horticultural ancestors did not know a thermophile from an enzyme, but *now* we do. *Because* we know, we can be taught to make better compost, with greater efficiency and accuracy than they.

3

Getting Down To Earth

EVEN today, compost piles have a bad reputation. In many places, it is still believed that they invite dogs and other pests, are the homes of mice, rats and snakes, and are iniquitous breeding dens for flies, mosquitoes and similar undesirable insects. Granted that dogs and rats may be a problem in some urban and suburban areas, the tales of devastation wrought by dogs and stories of rat-infested compost are grossly exaggerated. I have never seen a snake anywhere near a compost pile. Nor have we been plagued by bugs that were born out of our compost.

We have a frisky German shepherd bitch who, from the very beginning, along with a multitude of her friends, have all regarded our compost pile — when they have paid any attention to it at all — with intense boredom. We feed *her* our meat scraps and bones — not the pile. Chicken bones or fish bones, which she should not have anyway, are ground up fine and placed deep in the pile together with the other garbage. I am sure that if kitchen wastes were just thrown on top of the heap without being covered with a thick layer of hay, she would smell it, and be far more interested.

As it is, none of the neighborhood dogs has ever, to my knowledge, disturbed our compost pile at all. In fact, on a cold autumn night not long ago our shepherd was either too lazy to ask to come inside the house, or one of us was simply too lazy to let her in. As I was scraping frost from the car's windshield early the next morning, I heard the thump-thump of her tail and turned to see her returning my amused look from atop the warm compost pile, where she had apparently spent a comfortable night, without realizing there was something edible directly beneath her.

Fortunately, we have no rats around our place, but I am constantly trying to invent ways to outsmart a large tribe of raccoons that lives nearby and who raids our trash cans nightly. The dog and I both carry on a losing battle with them — I with assorted ropes, weights and other devices; she chiefly with loud nocturnal barking. She is particularly annoyed when they become bold enough to not only steal her dog food but wash it first in her water dish. The raccoons *are* forever in the trash, yet they seem to have no interest whatever in the compost. If you have something of a pest problem where you live, the difficulty can probably be resolved by some kind of cover, chicken wire perhaps, to protect your pile from them. More on that later.

LOCATION

In years past, people held rather strict Victorian attitudes towards composting. Whenever I see someone's compost pile tucked surreptitiously away in some corner of their property hidden by a screen or hedge, I am inevitably reminded of my great grandmother on my mother's side. One time my mother, as a young child, was sitting in a hallway as that fine lady made her grand exit from her marble bathroom. "Hi Grandma, have you been to the potty?" my mother asked. "My dear," replied my great-grandmother looking down, "Grandmothers *never* go to the bathroom!" In her day, undoubtedly, the "right sort" of people never made compost either.

Today, compost together with going to the bathroom, seem to have become more acceptable and less clandestine facts of life. In fact, such liberal attitudes have developed over the past couple of decades to a point where some members of the strictly organic school of gardening even regard their compost piles as a status symbol. Don't be ashamed of being a recycler. It is a more-than-honorable occupation. You need not *flaunt* the fact! It seems a little unnecessary — as happened to my wife and me recently — to take dinner guests by the hand and hustle them out to observe your compost heap. Your pile need not be in the most plainly visible spot on your land, but choose its locale carefully. There may be other factors to consider which are more important than appearance.

Obviously, you will want to have your compost pile as close as possible to the garden proper, so that you don't have to lug or cart materials back and forth over a long distance. If you own a pick-up truck or similar vehicle, which can help you bring in organic materials from other places, you should perhaps plan to build your composting system somewhere near a driveway or road. The pile does not need to be too near, or against the house itself. That seems a little *too* conspicuous. Moreover, you will not want it sitting directly under dripping eaves or downspouts which may dump an uncontrollable amount of water on it.

Your bin, box or pile *should* be somewhere near a water source, at least in a place your garden hose can reach. Some folks, because they worry about the chlorine in a municipal water system, go to great lengths to catch and collect pure rain water which they in turn use on their compost. I use chlorinated water all the time, both on my compost pile and on the garden, and must say that I have never noticed any ill effects. Chlorine *could* conceivably cause some damage to the microcommunity in the pile, but it is doubtful that much harm will be done to the microbial life there. If you really worry about it, neutralize the chlorine in the water by letting it sit in a container placed in the sun for a day or so before you use it.

Should your *pile* be placed in the sun or the shade? If you live in a cold climate and follow Leonard Wickenden's advice by warming it in the sun and increasing the microbiological activity within it, you run the risk of allowing the pile to dry out too easily and will have to keep watering it. If you build the pile in the shade, it won't dry out so quickly. But where I come from, shade usually implies shade *trees*. If the pile is not out in the open, some of the feeder roots from nearby trees may come in and help themselves to some of the goodness of the compost. This seems a little wasteful, especially if you already have healthy trees. You can't win either way, so choose the lesser of two evils.

You may also want to avoid a spot that is exposed to high winds. I live on a high, rather breezy bluff overlooking Lake Champlain. Sometimes, if the wind is just right, it can cause a bit of a mess. The other day a friend of mine, cool drink in hand, picked up a dried, partially decomposed cabbage leaf that had blown onto the lawn, and commented thoughtfully (as well as somewhat poetically), "Hmm. A compost pile in a windy place dries out and blows about."

A fairly standard bit of advice is that the pile should be protected on the north, east and west sides by some sort of wall, hedge or container, and that the south side, if possible, should be left open. I have never heard a really satisfactory explanation as to why this should be so I have never worried about it all that much. I have always assumed that this message was directed at people in the northern hemisphere and that composters in Argentina, South Africa and Australia, for instance, should keep the northern side of a retaining wall open.

The best reason for this would seem to be that the pile can be protected from cold winds, while at the same time the sun is allowed to reach it better and keep it warmer. This is a particularly good idea in some places, such as Alaska, where I understand it takes two to three years to make compost under the best circumstances. In most places, though, it can not be that important. Leave an opening in the side that seems most convenient for you.

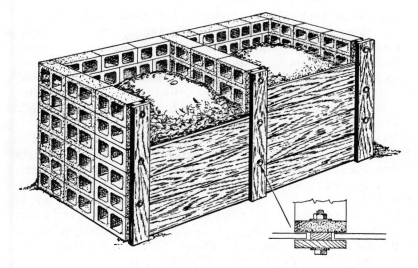

AN ELABORATE TWO-BIN COMPOST CON-
TAINER *made of wood and concrete blocks which are
held in place with mortar. The blocks are set on edge with
the holes open so that gases such as oxygen and carbon
dioxide can pass freely in and out of the compost. The
north side of the pile is protected from the cold wind by
hardwood boards which slide in and out of their vertical
tracks to allow easy access to the piles (see detail).*

Drainage can be something of a problem. I have often heard the
suggestion made that a pile should be located in a depression to
prevent the loss of nutrients through leaching. That sounds like a
good idea except that a low place often means standing water, or at
best, such good drainage under the soil in the depression that
nutrients are going to drain away anyway. In other words, if you want
your compost pile in a puddle, this is fine, but the result may be that
you end up with a smelly, anaerobic mess. I would say that ideally a
pile should be on a level spot where drainage is reasonably good.

Sticklers for neatness like to build their piles on concrete or
blacktop slabs. This not only provides a nice work space but it
prevents nutrients from being leached into the ground beneath the
pile. They may be right. I have always resented the thought that I was
fertilizing the earth under the pile rather than the garden itself. A slab
is a great idea so long as it is carefully built and not concave so that it

holds water. I still think it is better to have the pile in direct contact with bare ground. In fact, some people who agree with me dig down a couple of feet to establish the base of the pile. I wouldn't care to go that far, but I might dig up the sod and lay it aside for later use in, or on *top* of, the pile. The idea here is to give the microorganisms and earthworms maximum opportunity to find their way into the compost from the soil below. If you are too busy to dig up the sod, don't worry. It will have disappeared in a few months anyway.

Don't move your composting site around if you can help it. The longer a pile is in the same place the better. Composting takes less time when the ground is full of microbes, and keeping the pile in the same spot year after year will help the earth beneath to accumulate a large population of microorganisms and spores. When the pile is finally carted away to the garden to enrich the soil there, and a new pile is started, the remaining bacteria and fungi can start right in on it. It is not a bad idea to leave a little finished compost on the site to act as a "culture" for the new heap of organic matter.

COMPOST CONTAINERS

Many gardeners ask, "Why do I need a bin or a box; why not just a pile?" Good question. A pile works fine if you have the time and the patience to build it carefully, shape it properly, and can continue to keep it correctly shaped after you have turned it or added more materials. The main advantage of the container is that you don't have to waste time tapering the pile so that it doesn't become top-heavy and fall over. The container can be as complicated as you are handy and imaginative. Or it can be a very simple thing if you are too busy to make something more elaborate.

Most compost containers — "organizers" as they are sometimes called — are modifications of Sir Albert Howard's New Zealand compost box. Sir Albert suggested the design for the original box which was built by a gardening club in Auckland, New Zealand. Howard also very wisely suggested that *two* boxes side by side would yield the best results. His thought was that a gardener could be building a pile in one bin as materials became available to him while the second box, already filled with organic matter, was left to ferment.

The New Zealand box is made of wood. The design specifications, as were all of Howard's directions, are very precisely outlined. Besides assorted nuts, bolts and washers, you would need:

- 6 pieces of 2" x 2", x 3', 3" long for uprights.
- 24 pieces of 1" x 6" x 48" for the sides.

The uprights are to be driven into the ground to a depth of three inches. The sides, six boards to a side, are to be bolted to the uprights around three sides of where the pile was to be (see following illustration.). A ½ inch gap is to be left between each of the side boards to allow air into the pile.

The box has no top and no bottom and a removable front; the 1" x 6" boards there are not fastened by bolts, but can be slid in and out as needed, to permit access to the pile. The dimensions of the base are 4 feet by 4 feet. It is 3 feet high, and allows air circulation from all four sides. To keep the sides of the box from bulging out, Sir Albert recommended a cross bar with blocks on either end which would rest, unfastened, on top of the container.

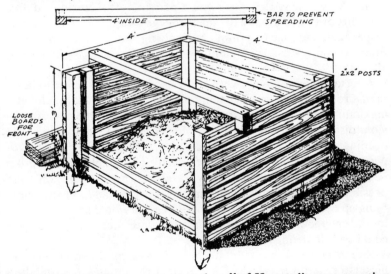

There is actually no reason to take *all* of Howard's very exacting instructions to heart. You should consider the New Zealand box as a frame of reference from which you can design your own container. The dimensions of 4 feet by 4 feet are good ones for any home composting system. But a pile which is slightly *higher* than three feet might be a little more desirable, as you will see shortly. Wood is a perfectly satisfactory building material. Cedar and cypress resist decay as well as any wood and will make a long-lasting box. So will redwood, although many conservationists and environmentalists would have strong objections to using lumber from that endangered species of tree.

Howard recognized that wood is biodegradable and saw a need for some sort of wood preservative. He realized that creosote and tar were items that should not be used because they would have a damaging effect on some of the organic matter in the pile and would be toxic to many microorganisms, insects, and earthworms. He recommended used motor oil as a preservative, which, to my way of thinking, is only slightly better than creosote. If you ever have a spot of ground where you want to be sure *nothing* will grow, empty the crankcase of your car there.

I have been told that Cuprinol, a well-known commercial wood preserver which comes in several colors, including green, is all right to paint on a wooden compost frame. I have never dared try it on anything that was going to be touching plants — even on a tomato trellis. Maybe it is the smell which puts me off. Cuprinol, unlike creosote, dries quickly and the smell *does* go away. Still, my nose tries to persuade me that Cuprinol and growing things should not mix. Epoxy or water-base latex paint would be safer, linseed oil safest of all.

A rectangular container with corner posts is a little easier to build than a round one. A circular bin, however, is ideal in that it allows a maximum amount of air to penetrate to all parts of the pile. An obvious disadvantage is the difficulty of making any kind of convenient opening in the circle. Leonard Wickenden, author of *Gardening With Nature,* suggests building a pile in the shape of a doughnut. This hole-in-the-middle design would allow for almost perfect aeration. One possible problem posed by the plan is that you would louse the whole thing up each time you had to turn the pile and would have to spend a lot of time rebuilding. Of course in a pile with such a shape, turning could be less frequent.

Round containers can be made with wire mesh, snow fencing, pickets or hardware cloth. For information about a free-standing circular compost organizer, write to the Garden Way Living Center, 1186 Williston Road, So. Burlington, Vermont 05401. Another good wire container, shaped like a box, with a cover to keep out raccoons, squirrels and other pests, is the Hold-All, manufactured by the Gilbert and Bennet Co., Georgetown, Connecticut 06829.

The easiest method of all — if you want your compost pile to be in the shade — seems to be to stretch some hardware cloth between several trees and staple it securely in place. I have seen containers made with field stone dry walls and have built containers myself out of cinder blocks. A stable four-foot block wall can be made easily without using any mortar. If you lay the blocks on their sides, the holes will provide excellent ventilation. The advantage of any stone or concrete block wall is that it retains heat from the sun and will keep the compost warm for a while as the air temperature drops.

Bales of hay make a good retainer, and the hay itself can be gradually incorporated into the pile. A bale of hay has a lot of insulation value. Rural folks in Vermont "bank" the foundations of their homes with bales in the fall to keep out the cold winter wind which will find its way through even the tiniest crack in a wall. Kill several birds with one stone: insulate your pile with bales, allow the hay to weather as it sits outside all winter (weathered hay, by the way, makes superior mulch), and keep a ready supply of new compost material right on the compost site.

Maybe you have a steep bank or hillside on your place which seems like wasted space. Try digging out a section of the side hill and building your pile there. This would be warm and invited to all sorts of beneficial insects, grubs, earthworms, bacteria and fungi. Aeration could be a problem though. This pile should be turned frequently. A short log-cabin type structure makes an attractive bin. Sod walls are another possibility. I have seen this work beautifully, but this kind of pile gets little air and needs to be turned often. You might try bricks or lattice work too. Use your imagination.

PILE STRUCTURE

Structuring your compost pile does *not* have to be done in an exact way. Don't let anyone tell you otherwise. Construct the pile as materials become available to you if you like. But you may have better luck if you try to accumulate a fairly sizable mass of organic matter before you begin. Autumn, as I mentioned earlier, is probably the most convenient time to start a new pile.

The base measurements of a pile are not that critical either. The pile can be as *long* as you want to make it. On the other hand, if you vary too much from Sir Albert's recommendation of 4 feet by 4 feet by making it much wider than 5 feet, the center of the pile may not get enough air and you will wind up with an anaerobic area there. Air naturally penetrates anywhere from 18 to 24 inches into a pile from all directions, but not much beyond that. It will also become more difficult to turn if it becomes too big.

Your compost pile should not be less than 2½ to 3 feet high if you have enough materials to make it higher. A pile that is too small will have a hard time heating up and will cool off, even freeze, quite readily. In most areas of the continental United States a compost pile needs quite a bit of mass — a volume of no less than a cubic yard — to be big enough to be self-insulating and maintain temperatures of 150 degrees Farenheit or more. A pile that is too low may lose its heat so quickly each night that pathogenic organisms, weed seeds and insect larvae are not exposed to high temperatures for a long enough period of time to be killed. By the same token, piles that get too *high* can get too heavy, which means that the lower levels of material get so compacted that they become airtight, and decay will be inhibited. A pile that is somewhere between 4 and 6 feet high is just about ideal.

If you have lots of material to start with, try to build your pile like a Dagwood sandwich, in many, many layers, using as many ingredients as you can get your hands on. Alternate "green" layers of fresh vegetable matter with "dry" layers of weathered material; "absorbent" layers with "wet" layers.

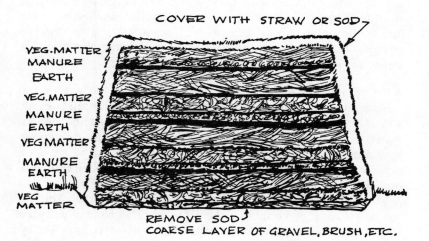

COVER WITH STRAW OR SOD

VEG. MATTER
MANURE
EARTH
VEG. MATTER
MANURE
EARTH
VEG MATTER
MANURE
EARTH
VEG MATTER

REMOVE SOD
COARSE LAYER OF GRAVEL, BRUSH, ETC.

The question arises as to whether you should intentionally allow *all* of your organic matter to weather, dry out and turn gray before adding it to the pile as some suggest. The "layer cake" or "sandwich" method allows and even encourages the use of both types of organic matter. Withered plant tissue contains little moisture and little nitrogen, and for this reason it is hard to break down. Green matter has both moisture and nitrogen in abundance and *it* will break down more rapidly. But a pile made only of green material may contain *too* much water, become soggy, and perhaps contain too *much* nitrogen. This is not a healthy situation either. Try to strike a good balance between the two. Your pile will have better ventilation, smell better and be more efficiént.

Some have suggested laying an impervious film of polyethylene plastic on the ground before starting to build a pile. The theory is that this will trap whatever nutrients may leach out of the pile. Certain nutrients, potassium (sometimes called potash) for example, will wash out of compost quite easily. But again: if by trying to retain a little potash (which can be easily replaced by adding wood ashes to the pile) you cut off the oxygen supply and make the pile less accessible to macroorganisms and microbes, you are in effect robbing Peter to pay Paul. Laying plastic also cuts off earthworms and, along with building a pile in a swamp or on a concrete slab, is a questionable practice.

Instead of polyethylene, try a layer of very coarse material — light brush or hedge trimmings, for example — as the very bottom layer of the pile. This will encourage aeration. But don't make this first layer so thick that it raises the pile off the ground. Too much air underneath can cool the pile too much. You might also discourage the immigration of earthworms. A good rule of thumb for compost making is to avoid having a layer of any one material more than six inches thick. Some very exacting composters notch or magic-marker the corner posts of a container in 6-inch increments so they will know exactly where they are as they build the pile.

Mix materials together as thoroughly as possible. Try not to let one kind of stuff get concentrated in any one portion of the pile. An old stand-by formula might be: a 6-inch layer of vegetable matter, a second layer of different vegetable matter, a layer of some sort of animal matter (usually manure), a thin layer of soil, a sprinkling of lime or limestone, then water, and repeat the process.

This formula can be easily adapted and changed. You may choose, after reading further, to leave out the soil, or lime, or both! You may not *have* any kind of animal matter, so you may decide to use another natural activator which will be described in Chapter 5. The one ingredient you cannot eliminate is water. Sprinkle the pile after you have built up a few layers so that all the organic matter is not drowned but has the consistency of a "wrung-out sponge."

As the pile approaches a height of around four and a half feet, begin to give some thought to insulation. You will have to make your pile bulkier if it is to function at optimum efficiency throughout the winter. The idea is to keep the pile as operational as possible for as long as possible during the coldest months. A heavy layer of straw, hay or leaves will save heat and slow down leaching.

A waterproof cover of some kind is okay. In fact, it might do a good job of keeping moisture *in* the pile. On the other hand, a piece of material such as plastic, well anchored on the ground, might inhibit the coming and going of air through the sides of the pile. A burlap or canvas "blanket" is almost as effective as leaves or straw. It will allow some water and gases through and still keep the pile warm. The important thing is to keep the fungi in the pile as warm as you can. Their growth, even more than that of bacteria, is greatly restricted by cold temperatures.

Maggots — fly larvae — can be a annoyance in some piles. Flies like to breed in damp hay or straw. This is why some people will lay screening over the insulative layer to keep the parent flies out. Others will cap a pile with a layer of sod or loose soil. Evidently, flies steer away from piles that are topped with dirt. The soil is also supposed to trap beneficial gases — nitrogen, for example, which might be escaping from the pile. On the negative side, soil on top allows weeds to establish themselves, while straw prevents them from growing there.

In either case, decide what shape you want the top of the pile to have. If you live in a very wet climate you may want the pile to be rounded. Remember how old-fashioned hay stacks were designed to shed excess water? Try doing the same thing. If it tends to be very dry where you live, especially during the summer, make the top of your pile concave — cupped or dished — so that it will trap and hold rain water which can later seep slowly into the pile.

To ensure good aeration in all parts of the heap, you might try standing on top of the pile and poking holes in it with the pointed end of a crowbar. Then if you like, push long loose bundles of cornstalks or straw into the holes. This solves the problem of such vent holes caving in. You can also make cylinders of chicken wire or hardware cloth. It is pretty hard to poke these chimneys down into a pile once it is built without bending them out of shape. It is easier to plan ahead and build the pile around them. The most effective ventilating stacks I have seen were lengths of perforated drainage pipe. This is the stuff that is laid beneath gravel around the perimeters of new houses. I call it Orangeburg or Bermco, which are probably trade names. The best thing about this substance is that you can force it down into the organic matter after the pile is complete.

VENTILATING STACKS

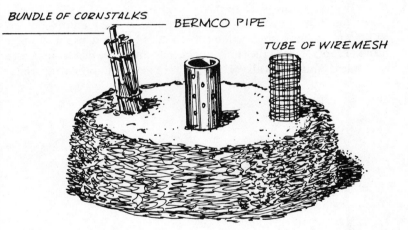

BUNDLE OF CORNSTALKS — BERMCO PIPE

TUBE OF WIREMESH

As decomposition really gets under way, the pile will shrink anywhere from 20 to 60 percent, depending on the state of the materials which have been put into it. Add new layers of material to increase the height again if you like. On the average, the weight of finished compost will equal half to three quarters the total weight of the original material. A cubic yard of finished compost, for example, weighs about one ton.

You will be amazed at how fast weeds may grow in your compost. Don't let them ambush the pile's water supply. Weed roots which will grow very close to the surface of the pile will intercept moisture before it has a chance to get to the material below.

This past spring a pole bean seed somehow found its way into the compost pile at our house. I planted seeds in the garden from a torn and leaky seed package on a Saturday, so it must have gotten there that day as I was getting some compost out of the pile to put under the bean hills.

When I returned a couple of days later — and this is no exaggeration — there, growing out of the pile, was a 12 inch high stem with tiny bean leaves at its top. As soon as I saw it, I dashed back into the house, all set to write a wonderful children's story called "Jack and the Beanstalk." My wife threw cold water on the whole thing by calmly reminding me that I was too late for that one. I have since found out after reading Sam Ogden's *Step by Step to Organic Vegetable Growing,* that I am actually not the first to think that the original inspiration for that fairy tale might have been a lowly compost pile and a pole bean seed.

The moral of my story: To avoid trouble with a giant or with an overly dry compost pile: pull out the weeds before they get too big; turn the roots toward the sun; and leave them on the pile to die. Once your pile is built, that's all you should have to worry about for a while.

4

Gourmet's Delight or Potluck?

I used to worry a lot about people who complained that they could never find enough organic matter to keep their garden soil in good shape, let alone accumulate enough to build a compost pile. That does *seem* like a problem in some particularly neat and well-kept city and suburban areas, but I don't worry so much any more. As Beatrice Trum Hunter points out, "Our industrialized society has created a far greater variety of organic materials than ever existed previously." And as someone else once said, "Where there's a will there's a way."

We should all try to recognize the abundance of existing "waste." It is the easiest thing in the world, as far as I can see, to find all sorts of available organic matter. You and I could, for instance, go out in my pick-up truck on any summer morning in Charlotte, Vermont and within two hours — and without going more than ten feet off the road — pick up enough materials like cut grass and weeds and leaves, to build *several* compost piles.

Granted: Charlotte is a rural community. You may have to go thirty, or even fifty feet off the road where you live. (And if you *do* venture that far afield, you'd better check to be sure that you are not trespassing and stealing something of value from someone's property.) In some cases, you may even have to seek out cheap sources of compostable material which you can *buy*. The point is that if you look for it a little, organic matter is still very easy to find.

The chances are that you will accumulate a lot of the same kind of

material all at once: leaves, or hay, or grass clippings. If you put a lot of dry hay on your pile without mixing it with something else, you may create a situation where you have too much carbonaceous material and not enough nitrogen in the pile. (The relationship between carbon and nitrogen will be explained in detail in Chapter 7.) Too many grass clippings will heat up all right, but they will probably form a slimy anaerobic mess. Too many leaves all at once will mat. As you gather organic materials, leave part of what you gather *off* the pile, but somewhere nearby, so that you can mix it with whatever materials you may pick up later.

As a composter, it is not only important to have some knowledge of the biological processes taking place within the pile. You should also know something about the organic ingredients you are putting into your mixture. The greater the variety of different things in the pile the better. This variety increases the chances of obtaining a nicely-balanced compost. The more diversified the mix, the more different' types of microorganisms will be at work.

It is possible that in some carefully controlled experimental situations, compost would be made according to precisely-measured formulas, so that exactly the same compost could be made over and over again. Under most ordinary circumstances, this is unnecessary. In fact, to my mind, it is more fun to take pot luck. If you are a novice, you may want to stick pretty close to the standard and very flexible rule of thumb for composting: two parts vegetable matter to one part animal matter.

Dead fish, dead animals and birds as well as manure, ground bones and scraps, all qualify as animal matter. You might even throw on a dead horse or cow if you happen to have one lying around and have a large enough pile. Actually, to be serious for a moment, be a *little* careful about this. Laws in many states — Vermont, for example, state that animal carcasses are to be buried underground. No one is going to arrest you, probably, for composting a few mice and a robin or two. But check out local ordinances and laws before you use the bodies of larger animals.

"Trash" fish as well as fish cleanings make good compost. This can include fresh water fish like suckers, rock bass, horned dace and many others. Go fishing for your compost pile as well as for your dinner table. No one will accuse you of being unsportsmanlike if you don't throw these fish back. Collect dead fish along shorelines and beaches too. Maybe you can get to them before they become really ripe and smelly. If you discover them before your dog does and has a chance to roll in them, you may avoid having to give him a bath later on, though with his more gifted nose he will nearly always beat you to the punch.

The supply of compostable materials is limitless. To be composted, a material need only have two characteristics: (1) It must be biodegradable, and (2) it must contain things which are usable and available to microorganisms. Here is a very incomplete list of such things:

A PARTIAL LIST OF MATERIALS SUITABLE FOR COMPOSTING

algae (pond weeds)
apple pomace (cider press
    waste)
artichoke leaves
ashes (from wood, corncobs,
    fruit skins etc.)
asparagus tops (chopped)
banana skins
bean shells
bean plants
beet tops
birdcage cleanings
broccoli stalks (shredded or
    or cut)
buckwheat hulls
buckwheat straw
cabbage stalks and outer
    leaves
cocoa hulls
carrot tops and scrappings
castor pomace
cat litter (pyrophyllite and
    vermiculite)
cauliflower leaves
citrus wastes and rinds
clover (red, green and sweet)

coffee wastes and grounds
corn cobs (shredded and
    chopped)
corn stalks (shredded)
cottonseed hulls
cotton waste ("gin trash")
cow peas
cucumber vines
dolomite
earthworms
eel grass
egg shells (ground or crushed)
feathers
felt waste
fish scraps (heads, tails,
    innards)
fish, "trash" (suckers, dace,
    etc.)
flowers
gelatine plant waste
grape pomace (winery waste)
granite dust
grass (rye, timothy, etc.)
grass clippings (lawn)
greensand
hair

hay (mixed grasses or salt
  marsh hay)
hedge clippings
hemp waste
hops, spent (brewery waste)
incinerator waste (less metal
  and other nonbiodegradable
  matter)
kelp (seaweed)
kitchen refuse (less animal fat)
leaf mold
leather waste and dust
leaves (all varieties)
lettuce
lime (agricultural)
limestone (ground)
marble dust

milk (sour — whole or skim)
muck (marsh and swamp mud,
  dried)
muskmelon (vines, leaves and
  rinds)
olive residues
oat straw
peanut hulls
pea waste (pods and vines)
peat moss
phosphate rock
phosphorous (superphosphate)
pine needles (white, red, cedar,
  etc.)
potash rock
potato wastes (leaves, stalks
  and skins)

rhubarb leaves
rice hulls
sawdust (weathered, hardwood
and soft)
shavings, wood
shells, ground (clam, crab,
lobster, mussle, oyster, etc.)
silk mill waste
sludge (processed sewage —
where suitable)
squash waste (vines, leaves)
soybean straw
sphagnum moss
sugar cane residue (bagasse)
takage (slaughter house refuse)

tannery waste
tea leaves
tobacco waste (stalks and
stems)
tomato plants and stems
turnip tops (rutabaga tops)
vetch
watermelon waste (vines,
leaves and rinds)
weeds
wheat straw
whey
wood chips
wool (waste and rags)

SOME COMMONLY-USED MATERIALS

It is not within the scope of this book to discuss in detail each of the items in this abbreviated list. You know far better than I what compostable materials are easy to find near your home. If you don't know, you should make an effort to find out.

It is worth touching on a few items of particular interest and mentioning some of the things you are most likely to get your hands on without spending a great deal of time and money.

Ashes

Incinerator ashes and burned charcoal are probably not worth composting, but wood ashes from a fireplace or stove are valuable to any gardener, especially if they are sifted through a screen to get rid of large particles of charcoal. Wood ashes are a source of potash. Some organic gardeners use them as a pest deterrent. I am told, for instance, that if they are sprinkled on cabbages they will discourage cabbage worms. A fine sprinkling of wood ashes can also be put into the compost pile, once every eighteen inches or so, and then covered with more organic matter.

Wood ashes lose a lot of their value if exposed to a soaking rain, because the potash leaches out of them very easily. This is why *many* layers of ashes is a good idea. Burning the skins of certain fruits and vegetables is a common practice among some purely organic gardeners. Ashes from banana skins, lemon skins, cucumbers and cocoa shells have a very high phosphorous and potassium content.

Feathers

Pluckings from chickens, turkeys and other fowl should be saved and composted. Feathers contain a large amount of nitrogen.

Garbage

Almost all organic kitchen refuse is excellent compost material. There are some notable exceptions: grease, oil and animal fat — commonly known these days as *cholesterol.* The compost pile seems to have as much trouble breaking down fat as the human body does. Bacon fat, for instance, thrown onto the pile when it is still liquid, can coat the fibers of some materials and preserve them almost as if they were varnished.

Grass Clippings

A pile composed entirely of grass clippings looks fine on the surface, but the dry, brown outer veneer is usually only about half an inch thick. Underneath, you are likely to find a homogeneously odorous mess which is a particularly attractive breeding ground for flies. If you have grass clippings in great abundance — as many of us do— do one of three things: (1) Dry them before putting them on the pile; (2) mix them with some other dry and absorbant material while they are still green, (green clippings will help the pile to heat up quickly); or (3) put them into your layer-cake pile in *very* thin layers.

Ground stone and shells

Rocks and shells of course contain many minerals needed by plants. But it is awfully hard to dissolve a large stone, especially in plain water. Vermont is fortunate to have many quarries, making it easy for us to get stone dust. Granite or marble dust for example, that has been pulverized into very *fine* particles will dissolve fairly quickly in any moist compost pile. By the time the compost is complete, many of these minerals are ready to be assimilated by plants. Ground oyster, clam, and lobster shells, to name just a few, will do the same thing. Pulverized oyster shells, by the way, is a fine lime substitute.

Hay or Straw

Dried hay or straw — if it is going to make up a large percentage of the pile — should be weathered first. The most compostable types of hay are those which have been left in a field, have turned grey, and are "spoiled" — which only means that the hay is unfit for livestock feed. In many cases, a farmer is happy to get rid of this stuff at very little cost to you.

Unweathered straw or hay requires a tremendous amount of nitrogen if it is going to decay. In their efforts to break it down, bacteria may use up all of the existing nitrogen in a compost pile and still not have enough to do a thorough job. If you find the explanation of the carbon-nitrogen ratio (see Chapter 7) too complicated to understand, or you forsee some difficulty in making the proper *adjustments* in that ratio, it might be wise to use unweathered hay and straw in only very small amounts.

Hedge trimmings

Hedge trimmings and branches pruned from trees are usually very coarse and difficult to break down unless they are chopped or shredded. But an occasional layer of unchopped hedge trimmings *can* be used in the pile. They make good "roughage" and will permit air penetration. Don't overdo it though, or your finished compost may be full of little undecomposed twigs.

Hops

Spent hops — brewery waste — make rich compost even though they may have a beery smell for a while. A word of caution about hops: they are apt to be quite wet when you get them, and will retain much of this moisture. A pile with lots of spent hops will not need to be watered very often. Keep checking to see that your pile is not overly moist. A pile that becomes too wet, of course, needs to be turned.

Leaves

Native Vermonters are sometimes amused by the "leaf freaks" who invade our state each autumn to enjoy the brilliant foliage. As a composter you should become a "leaf freak" too. But learn to appreciate leaves for their nutritive qualities as well as for their esthetic ones. Deep tree roots do a fine job of retrieving trace elements from deep in the subsoil. The roots then give these minerals back to the leaves for temporary storage. *Harvest* leaves. Throwing them away is one of the worst kinds of conspicuous waste I know of.

To be perfectly honest, leaves *will* break down quite slowly. A pile of leaves with nothing added may sit for years before it will be completely decomposed. Yet, they should be an important part of anybody's compost pile. The chemical make-up of partially-rotted leaves — *leaf mold* as it is called — is perhaps the closest thing in nature to pure humus. If you chop leaves and mix them with other things, they will decompose about four times as fast as they would normally.

If you *don't* chop them they can mat, cake together and prevent aeration whenever they get wet. If you can not buy, borrow or rent a chopper to use, play it safe with leaves by building them into the pile in fairly thin, fairly dry layers. Oak or beech leaves, incidentally, if used exclusively, will make a slightly acidic compost, good for rhododendrons and blueberries.

Leather waste

If you can get it, leather dust is very high in nitrogen and phosphorous. This is very plentiful and inexpensive in some places.

Pine needles

Pine needles, including red and white pine, as well as cedar, break down fairly slowly in a compost pile. They should be considered a good compost texturizer but should rarely be considered a major ingredient. They, like peat moss, oak leaves and beech leaves, tend to make the pile slightly more acidic, but this should not necessarily be thought of as a negative quality, because the rest of the materials may neutralize whatever acid effect they have.

Peat moss

I have long felt that peat moss is an over-rated and over-priced gardening material. Peat adds almost nothing to your pile in terms of nutrient value, and if it is allowed to get too concentrated in one part of the pile, it can absorb all of the moisture there, leaving the rest of the pile high and dry. Mixed thoroughly with other stuff, on the other hand, it makes a marvelous texturizer and conditioner for the compost, because it rots so much slower than nearly everything else. After all, if everything were to disintegrate at the same speed, all of the particles of organic matter would be the same size, and your compost would have a uniform but less desirable consistency.

Sawdust

Sawdust should be worked into the pile in very thin sprinklings. If *it* gets too concentrated it will break down *very* slowly, and if it is very powdery may form an airtight seal to boot. The ideal way to compost sawdust is to sandwich it between layers of manure. Oddly enough, softwood sawdusts (pine, spruce, cedar etc.) break down much more slowly than hardwood sawdusts (maple, oak, birch and so on). Weathered sawdust decomposes much more readily than fresh.

Seaweed (kelp)

I was surprised to learn that many kinds of seaweed have no cellulose. It rots quite easily as a result and can be mixed with something that has a lot of bulk, such as straw. Seaweed, as many gardeners have said, contains "lots of goodies": boron, iodine,

calcium, magnesium, sodium and other trace elements. It may be easy to get too *many* "goodies", particularly sodium, from seaweed. If it is to be put directly on the garden in large amounts, this should be done only about once every three or four years. We haven't yet figured out exactly *what* percentage of an average compost pile should be composed of seaweed, but I have been assured that it is nothing to worry about so long as the *majority* of the pile is not kelp.

One gardener I know maintains that a thick blanket of seaweed is better than anything else — organic or artificial — for keeping a pile well insulated in wintertime.

Sludge

I have had trouble deciding whether or not to put "sludge," the product of a sewage treatment plant, under the heading of "Materials to Avoid". It might *also* be considered an activator. Human excrement, we know, contains pathogenic bacteria and parasites which require a lot of heat to kill — in some cases more heat than a normal pile will generate. We could, undoubtedly, learn a great deal from the Chinese who apparently compost raw human excrement safely and have been doing so successfully for centuries. Some devices are being developed which are designed to compost sewage right in the home. I will describe one in the "Alternatives" chapter.

Sludge may *also* have some pathogens. To make matters worse it may contain excessive amounts of zinc, copper, cadmium, corrosive acids, nonbiodegradable detergents, pesticides and insecticides such as DDT. If you were to use sludge in your compost pile and were to use this compost for growing vegetables, these harmful substances would wind up in your garden plants, and ultimately in your own body.

Sewage sludge poses a special problem. On one hand, we should all encourage the building of sewage treatment plants and make every effort to find ways of using the product; on the other, some warning about its use in the garden or compost pile still seems necessary. Firm conclusions about sludge seem to lie somewhere near the elusive solution to the problem of water pollution. If all the dangerous substances other than sewage itself could be removed from our streams and waterways, we could probably produce a safer, more usable sludge.

As it stands now, *activated* sludge is the product which, although it may contain some harmful chemicals, is high in nitrogen and almost totally free of pathogens. It is sometimes packaged and sold in a dried form under the name "Milorganite." A kind man at a nearby sewage treatment plant once patiently explained to me that activated sludge is safe to compost *or* to use as mulch. He did advise, however, that to be *perfectly* safe, even activated sludge should sit around for at least a year after it is processed if it is going to be used as a mulch for root crops such as beets, carrots, turnips and others.

Digested sludge should *not* be used in a home compost pile. It is the result of an anaerobic treatment process which only destroys *most* of the pathogenic bacteria. Some of the ones that remain *might* be killed in the normal heating of a compost pile, but there is a very good chance that they would not be.

Sod

In one shot, sod should add both loam (good topsoil) *and* organic matter to your compost. But don't dig up turf from somewhere and throw it into the pile in one big clump. Distribute it throughout some of the material that is already there. Sod is a splendid insulator, and as I suggested earlier, should keep flies away. Try covering the top of your pile with sod — roots up, grass down. If you do this in the fall, by spring the sod will have disappeared.

Weeds

I stopped to see a friend not long ago, just as he had finished weeding his garden. He had all of the weeds neatly packed in boxes ready to be taken to the dump. Most of the weeds he had pulled had already gone to seed. Fearing that by tilling them directly back into the garden between his rows he would only be propagating the various weed species, he had elected to sacrifice the organic matter they contained in the hope of saving himself some work later on. I didn't tell him so, but I couldn't help thinking that with a good active compost pile he could have had his cake and eaten it too.

He could have kept the organic matter and allowed the pile to "thermal kill" the weed seeds. Once exposed to the temperatures at which thermophilic bacteria operate, most weed seeds cannot survive for long. But there are other ways that weed seeds can be done in. I understand that a seed subjected to the digestive system of an earthworm can never germinate.

If you add weeds to your pile, remember: the more weed seeds, the more need for manure or some other nitrogen-rich material to *ensure* sufficient heating. Weeds that have gone to seed should be put near the center of the pile where the heat is most intense. If you just leave them on the surface of the pile some seeds will germinate and begin to grow there.

Composting weeds can save you work in another way too. There is no need to shake all of the dirt off the roots. Adding soil to the heap will *improve* the compost. In fact, soil is one of the very best natural activators.

Don't forget about wool, cotton and silk rags, carpet sweepings, hair, and material from the vacuum cleaner. Even old wool trousers will decompose, as I was reminded recently, if they are cut into small pieces and wet. Some modern synthetic fabrics, unfortunately, do not rot so readily — some not at all.

STUBBORN MATERIALS

Corn cobs, apple pomace (even though it smells nice), cotton stalks, sugar cane leaves (*not* bagasse which is the cane residue), and palm fronds all are on the list of vegetable materials which are hardest to rot. To help them along, they should be mixed with stuff that easily will break down. If possible, they should be chopped too.

Cornstalks and husks are nearly as opposed to being decayed as are the cobs. The best and safest way to deal with them — and prevent corn diseases — is to till them under the soil. If you are going to leave them above ground, it is probably safe to say that they *must* be run through a shredder if they are to be composted at all efficiently. Apple pomace, like spent hops, contains lots of moisture and should be spread in thin layers. Also the apple seeds in it seem to have a great resistance to heat. They may survive until after the pile is cooled and then become an enticement to mice and other rodents.

Peanut hulls decompose quite easily and contribute lots of nitrogen. Walnut, pecan and almond shells, on the other hand, break down *very* slowly. They, like stone, contain many important minerals. A good chopper can pulverize them enough so that they will rot in a fraction of the time it would normally take for them to decay. Wood chips also take a long time to break down unless they are chopped quite fine. It may take as long as a couple of years to compost some woody materials completely.

Thalassa Cruso, in *Making Things Grow Outdoors,* reminds us that prickly things like rose bushes and raspberry canes can produce a thorny problem. Thorns themselves, it seems, are so hard that they resist decomposition and are too small to be effectively chopped by a machine. The cane will rot fine, but the thorns might lie peacefully in the pile waiting for a chance to rise up and attack you as you are handling the compost later.

In *The Organic Gardener,* Kit Foster claims that she likes to compost "cage cleanings and shredded junk mail." What *about* paper? It accounts for about fifty percent of the household waste in most families. It *is* mostly organic matter. Some argue that printer's ink contains some beneficial trace elements, while others say that it is toxic to plants. Most agree that paper improves the *structure* of your compost, but that it should never be used in excess since it is extremely resistant to microbial attack. That seems like good advice. Regardless of how much you use, any paper headed for the compost pile should be shredded or, at the very least, scrunched up — never laid flat in sheets.

Newsprint is largely composed of lignin (wood fiber as you'll remember) which is one reason why it is so difficult to break down. Tough as it is, newspaper will rot quite quickly if mixed with some sort of "hot" manure like poultry litter. Other kinds of glossy paper resist even this. Waxed paper *never* seems to decompose. Scientists, fortunately, are working on the problem of waste paper. We should see more and more biodegradable paper before too many more years. Just recently I was looking a a piece of stationary from the Rodale Press, the publishers of *Organic Gardening and Farming* magazine. The paper was, as it said, "Made of 100% recycled paper." Whether or not recycled paper rots more easily than paper made from fresh wood pulp remains to be seen. I doubt that it does.

CHEMICALS

It is usually easier, if you are going to use them, to apply chemicals directly to the garden soil rather than put them through a composting cycle where they may be partially or even totally lost. Yet some people with greenhouses like to make "complete" potting compounds consisting largely of carefully made compost.

What minerals can be added to the pile to make a more perfectly balanced compost? How you might (or might *not*) add lime, limestone or lime substitutes to alter the acidity or alkalinity of your compost will be discussed later. For now, let me say that by adding lime, dolomite or wood ashes you are also adding *calcium,* an important trace mineral.

Basically, *nitrogen* gets into a heap in two ways: (1) "Nitrogen-fixing" bacteria, *azobacteria,* take nitrogen from the atmosphere and change it into a form which can be used by other microbes in the pile. (2) Nitrogen also gets into the pile in the form of protein which is contained in animal matter and in much vegetable matter.

It is pretty hard to get *phosphorous* into the pile organically, unless you add pure rock phosphate. Phosphorous, along with nitrogen and potassium, is considered to be one of the three elements vital to all plant growth. Your best bet, if you think that your compost *needs* phosphorous (or if tests show that it does), is to use "superphosphate" fertilizer (0-20-0). Superphosphate also contains some sulfur which, if it appears in very small amounts, is helpful to plants.

Wood ashes are one traditional source of *potassium.* Others are green sand and granite dust. The organic way may be the best means of getting potash into your compost. Adding potassium chloride is another possibility. So is muriate of potash. Magnesium chloride is another good chemical source of *many* trace elements. In most cases, though, a wide variety of organic matter will provide a sufficient number of necessary minerals.

MATERIALS TO AVOID

You might be tempted someday, when your pile has shrunk and looks disappointingly small, to "beef up" the volume of your heap by adding soil other than good loam or humus, which might help activate the pile. Mud, sand and gravel add very little to either the nutrient or bacterial value of compost, so leave them out.

I have stumbled on a leaflet put out by the Irish Department of Agriculture and Fisheries in Dublin which is called, simply enough, "Compost." The Irish, who should know about as much as anyone in the world when it comes to growing potatoes, are nervous about certain plant debris which could contain disease organisms that *might* have a chance of surviving the "thermal kill" of the composting process. They warn that potato tubers affected by wart disease and potato stalks invaded by *sclerotia* (dark, flattish bodies which indicate stalk disease), should not be thrown directly into the pile. A Potato Famine in one's national background would make a people understandably cautious about such things.

They also tell us to beware specifically of cabbage that has been affected by club root, root crops suffering from dry rot, celery leaves affected by leaf spot or blight, and onions that have been attacked by onion mildew. It takes an ideal compost system, they say, to provide the conditions necessary to *surely* destroy the pathogenic organisms which cause these diseases. Any vegetable matter that is questionable in this respect should be burned, especially if you are doubtful about your pile's ability to heat up enough. The ashes, then, should be perfectly safe, and *can* be added to the pile.

Most ashes are safe to mix into your compost heap. But coal ashes are not. They have *excessive* amounts of both sulfur and iron, amounts which are toxic to plants. Charcoal should be avoided too. This is something that many of us have a lot of because we use charcoal "bricquets" for outdoor cooking. The temptation is to throw partially burned charcoal on the compost pile. I have tried it. Months later I found that it had not decayed at all. No wonder. Archaeologists have discovered on more than one occasion that charcoal, which is primarily carbon, will resist decay even after thousands of years. Charcoal, perfectly preserved, has been discovered in the excavated ruins of many ancient peoples.

It used to be that you could compost nearly any kind of old fabric or rags. Today, an organic garment seems more the exception than the rule. Most clothes are now made wholly or partially from synthetic materials like nylon, rayon, dacron, and plastic. These are all nonbiodegradable. I am sure I don't need to remind you to keep *all* nonbiodegradable substances, including plastic, glass and aluminum objects, out of your compost heap. It is not that they will do any particular harm there. They will never do any *good*. Real rubber is organic in origin, but is slow to rot. Don't try to compost it.

I have heard that some people put insecticides, pesticides or poisons in their piles to keep insects and annoying animals out. This *is* harmful! This kind of thing seems to me to be just another manifestation of our preoccupation in this country with cleanliness and sterilization. Adding such things to your pile does little more than *seriously* disrupt the microcommunity there.

I am all in favor of people using low toxicity insecticides such as rotenone on their *gardens* whenever serious infestation occurs. But an insecticide like DDT, as you have no doubt heard, seems to persist and never disintegrates. Poisons of this sort are *forcing* us all to become more considerate neighbors whether we live in Greenland or Ceylon. Whether you like the idea or not, if your "neighbor" in Montana uses DDT, the chances of *your* being affected by it in Louisiana are quite high! We would all be smart to cool it with strong chemicals.

5

Special Ingredients —
Activators

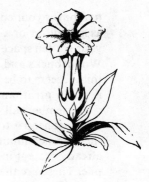

D ON'T forget that, given enough time, any biodegradable material will eventually rot. We have learned something about some of the things that could go into a composting system to make up the bulk of the final product. Now we need to think about some sort of activator, a catalyst or "starter" that will get things going microbiologically, an accelerator that can expedite the natural decomposition process. These are more than special ingredients which add "sugar and spice" to the compost. They are vital elements — simple as they may be — in the potluck recipe you are concocting. Trying to make good compost without an activator is like trying to make concrete without cement.

One of history's earliest records having to do with gardening tells us that the ancient Babylonians used the blood from camels and other creatures (one source tells us that they preferred human blood) as compost activator. Barbaric as this may seem to a squeamish twentieth-century mind, it should be noted that a great many successful composters use dried blood or blood meal — which is collected at slaughterhouses, dried and packaged — as a compost activator today. I have used it myself. As long as it is dry, it is nearly odorless and clean. It is no more than a very dark red, almost black powdery substance. I had no qualms at all about picking it out of the bag with my bare hands and throwing it on the pile.

This is not to suggest that you should worry about getting *your* hands on anything as exotic or expensive as blood meal to use as activator for your compost. If you *do* it, it can be put to even better use as a fertilizer or a pest repellent. Sprinkle some around the edges of your garden space or right in the rows among young beans and peas. Woodchucks and rabbits, who love nibbling on such tender young things, seem to be frightened by its scent. Dogs, unfortunately, think it smells great, and will do their best to lick it up.

Remember: all you are trying to do by adding activator to your compost heap is to provide a nitrogen-protein source which will feed the microcommunity. A carbon source and vitamin supply are already present in the other organic materials which will go into the pile. These are the three things — nitrogen, carbon and vitamins, as you will remember — that microorganisms need in order to grow and multiply. Once they begin working and reproducing themselves, your compost pile is functioning at near top efficiency.

ARTIFICIAL ACTIVATORS

There are certain chemicals — if you are into using such things — that can be used to bring up the nitrogen level of the compost pile. You might use a "complete" fertilizer such as 10-5-10. A typical composting formula would be to use one full cup of fertilizer for every ten square feet of level pile surface. This could be applied again each time your pile rose to a new height of six inches. You could also use ammonium sulfate, calcium nitrate or sodium nitrate in slightly lesser amounts. These will tend to leave a faintly acidic residue in the pile, but this "sourness" can be easily neutralized by adding some alkaline material like lime (see Chapter 7 on pH).

Some gardeners add fertilizers such as superphosphate or muriate of potash to their compost-in-the-making. A few of those I have talked to are slightly confused, thinking that such things will help to activate the dormant bacteria and fungi that are already in the pile. Unfortunately, "that ain't so." They *may* be helping to produce a more perfectly *balanced* compost because the phosphorous and potassium will go unused by the microorganisms — which are totally disinterested in these nutrients — and *might* remain held in the compost for later use by the garden plants.

In general though, chemical fertilizer is not particularly effective as an activator because it contains no protein the way animal matter and some vegetable matter does. In fact, chemicals will probably be more valuable if applied to compost after it is finished, (the "goodies" are less likely to be leached out that way), or to the garden soil directly. Then again, if you have some old fertilizer lying around that you don't know what to do with, there is no harm in throwing some on the compost heap.

Many commercial compost "starters" or so-called activators that we have tested prove to be little more than fertilizers which have been repackaged and marked up several hundred percent in price.

BACTERIAL ACTIVATORS

Bacterial activators, inoculants as they are sometimes called, usually consist of granules or tablets made up of a substance which includes dormant bacteria and fungi. The theory behind using them is that they introduce the proper microorganisms into the pile and assure a very rapid and satisfactory decomposition. A well known American inoculant is made by the Judd Ringer Company of Eden Prairie, Minnesota. Adco and Q. R. (Quick Return) are two British products which are said to "stimulate" and "support" bacterial growth. There is also the B.D. (Bio-Dynamic) Compost Starter from the Pfeiffer Foundation in Spring Valley, N.Y. This looks like brown dust, and I am not sure what it contains.

I have tried the bacterial activator that comes in the form of effervescent tablets, each of which are meant to be dissolved in one gallon of water. The tablet looks and acts something like an Alka-Seltzer. I kept a gallon of water-activator mixture around the house and each day would put some of it in my old kitchen blender which I use to grind up kitchen refuse before I threw it on the compost pile. Every time a quart or so of garbage was ground up, millions of the right bacteria should have been added and thoroughly distributed throughout the material. Once on the pile it was hard for my unscientific eye to see that this stuff was rotting any faster than other garbage that had passed through the blender and was mixed with plain water.

As already suggested in Chapter II, composting will be a whole lot simpler for you if you acknowledge the fact that the right bacteria, fungi and actinomycetes *already* exist within your compost pile. The potential for excellent decomposition is right there. Let Mother Nature worry about adjusting the various populations within the microcommunity. That's her job, and she does it well.

You will gain little time — certainly no more than a few hours — by introducing commercially packaged microbes into your system. A very high percentage of those you *do* bring in will probably not be the right ones anyway, as I have also said. Try some "natural" activator instead. They are cheaper — even free in some cases — and should work every bit as well. Remember that *your* only job is to set the stewing process in motion.

NATURAL ACTIVATORS

Here is a partial list of readily available materials high in nitrogen and protein content. If one or more of these is distributed throughout the other matter in the pile, you can be reasonably sure that you have activated your system.

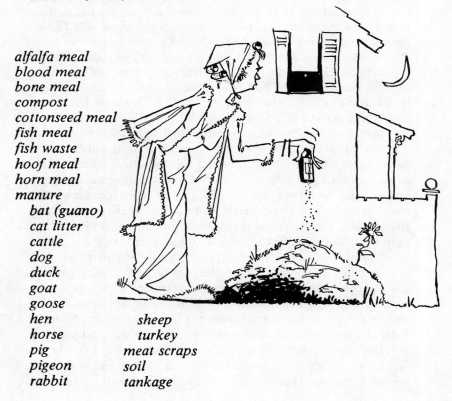

alfalfa meal
blood meal
bone meal
compost
cottonseed meal
fish meal
fish waste
hoof meal
horn meal
manure
  bat (guano)
  cat litter
  cattle
  dog
  duck
  goat
  goose
  hen   *sheep*
  horse   *turkey*
  pig   *meat scraps*
  pigeon   *soil*
  rabbit   *tankage*

One of the best activators is what is sometimes called "seeding compost." This is no more than "ripe" or finished compost which is left over or borrowed from another pile. A little of this will supply the new material with all kinds of microorganisms and possibly even a few earthworms which can become the founding fathers of a new colony. A two-inch layer of seeding compost can be put into your pile on top of every twelve inches or so of new organic matter.

Some folks like to douse their heaps with strong compost or rich-soil "tea". This can be easily brewed simply by filling a burlap or cheesecloth bag with good earth or compost and letting it sit in a bucket or barrel of water for several days. The darkened liquid which results is a good compost activator and an even better sidedressing for droopy plants that seem to need a quick boost.

Soil itself is teeming with microbial life. The best kind of soil to use as an activator is what you and I know as "loam." Loam is a fortunate mixture of sand, silt, clay and decaying organic matter. You can use it in layers about two inches thick — one layer of soil for every six inches or so of other matter.

It is probably a good idea *not* to take soil from a field or orchard where poisonous herbicide sprays and insecticides have been used. Such things, as you already know, remain in the earth for some time, and do not do the bacteria any good. Soil from the woods might be all right. It might also prove to be quite acidic — which lime will cure. Muck — that black soil dug out of swampy areas — is also good stuff for activating a pile. The Chinese — "farmers for forty centuries" — have used wet mud from canal bottoms.

Fresh stable manure may contain as much as 80% water. It should be allowed to dry out a bit so that it will not affect the water content of the pile or cut off the free passage of air to and from the different layers in the heap. All manures, like human excrement, have a very high bacteria count. Not all of the different strains of bacteria which come from a cow's intestines, for example, will actually *benefit* the compost. Most of them, in fact, will die as they are muscled out by the growth of other strains which are reproducing more efficiently. None of the bacteria in manure from healthy animals should be considered as dangerous pathogens. The only manure we have to fear is our own, and fortunately lots of capable people are working on ways to make *it* safe, as we shall see in Chapter 8.

Manures from horses, sheep and poultry are sometimes called "hot manures." If they are used when they are too fresh they can stimulate such frenzied bacterial activity that many of the pile's beneficial microorganisms are killed along with the harmful ones. Hot manures quickly inspire the generation of enough intense heat to cook the living daylights out of earthworms and other macroorganisms that have the misfortune or poor sense to hang around near the center of the pile.

Poultry manure seems to be one of the most potent activators there is. It will really warm things up in a hurry. Newspaper in fact — one of those "stubborn materials" mentioned in the last chapter — will decompose much more quickly if chicken, goose, or duck manure is added to it. Poultry manure should be — and almost always is — diluted and weakened by the addition of litter, which usually consists of sawdust, shavings or chopped straw.

The term "well-rotted manure" is used so often in gardening literature that it has become a cliché. Overworked expression or not, "well rotted manure" is the safest kind to use in the compost heap. It is usually lighter in color than fresh manure, drier and not nearly as smelly. There are literally tons of this stuff in rural areas, particularly in the spring after farmers have been emptying out their barns all winter. They will usually sell it cheap if you are willing to load it and cart it home yourself. If you have animals of your own, collect their droppings and leave them exposed to the weather for a few weeks before using them in the compost heap.

When we really want to make up a batch of compost and are not interested in experimenting with different techniques and materials, we are most likely to activate the piles with alfalfa meal — which almost always seems to be the expedient thing to do. Alfalfa meal *is* somewhat expensive, but is less so than blood meal, fish meal, hoof or horn meal. It is pleasant to smell and handle and is easy to get here in northern New England. If we were located elsewhere we might use cottonseed meal which works equally well. It is the simplest thing in the world to activate your pile with any kind of protein meal. Just add a heavy sprinkling to the pile every six inches or so, add water, and within forty-eight hours — I guarantee — your heap will be warm in the center.

An associate of ours was invited to a neighboring town not too long ago to give a short talk on vegetable gardening and composting. He loaded all sorts of gardening tools and paraphernalia into the back of a pick-up truck and took off for Lyndonville, Vermont. When he arrived he discovered that he had forgotten to bring along anything for activating the demonstration compost pile he had planned to build. Rather than panic, he went to the nearest grocery store, bought a fifty-pound bag of dry dog food, returned, and later sprinkled layers of it into the pile. Most dog foods contain meal — except the ones whose manufacturers insist otherwise, of course — and are, quite naturally, packed with protein. That was a pretty expensive compost made in Lyndonville that day, but some of the local people say that it was just great when it was finished.

One last thing about compost activators: Last year, I kept hearing an early morning radio commercial from a nearby grain company advertising "liquid protein." I called up and asked them what it was. "32% pure protein," the man said. "Feed it to cows. Helps their digestion." I asked if I could buy ten gallons to experiment with. "Ten gallons!" he roared, "You only got one cow? We sell this stuff by the truckload." I explained that we were interested in seeing if it would work as a compost starter, that I had no intention of making his company deliver the product to us, and that I would be happy to pick it up myself.

He just said, "O.K." on the phone, but when I got there with my two five gallon containers he was most helpful, answering all of my questions about Mol Mix 32-050 Liquid Protein and giving me literature which had a complete analysis listing the multitude of trace elements in the mixture. He charged me $1.50, asked a few quick questions about composting — some of which I could answer, some of which I could not — and sent me on my way.

Later, I thinned some of the heavy molasses mixture with water and built a compost pile out of some material which I thought would be particularly difficult to compost — brush chips which had been run through our shredder. To these I added some green and withered leaves and a few wood ashes. I put down four inches of chips and leaves, then a sprinkling of ashes and added the diluted liquid protein mixture. Then the pile was sprayed with a hose and another sandwich built on top. I continued this procedure until the pile was about four feet high in a wire mesh container. I used about five gallons of the pure Mol Mix which may have been too much. It was sticky and ran down the sides of the container the way maple syrup does, but otherwise it was easy to handle. It rinsed off my hands with plain cold water.

I stuck a probe thermometer into the pile, and in less than two days it registered 145 degrees. I doubt very much that finely textured compost can be made from brush chips in much less than a couple of years, but as an activator the liquid protein obviously worked fine. In fact, all of the things mentioned in this chapter work beautifully. That is why I have recommended them. It ought to be easy for you to get hold of at least one of the items on the list of natural activators.

6

Some of the Humdrum Mechanics

OMPOSTING can be a fascinating diversion — *most* of the time. If you are like me you may find it almost impossible *not* to visit your compost pile each day, push some of the top material aside, and have a look at what is going on inside. This sort of fascination is a kind of addiction, I guess, but a healthy one as far as the natural order of things is concerned.

The other day a self-sufficient neighbor of mine (who grows almost all of his own food to feed a family of five) was telling me about his father, a well known figure in New York publishing circles. He is totally unlike his son in that he is completely dependent on the supermarket for food and other necessities. "I don't think Dad has ever grown a vegetable in his life. He doesn't have the time or the space, really. But he has always been interested in gardening. He's been giving me books about it ever since I was about six. And, you know, for as long as I can remember he has always had a compost pile in his little back yard!" I wondered what he did with all his compost once it was finished. My friend replied, "I think he gives it to a neighbor who grows championship roses." This man is a purist — one of the most dedicated composters I have ever heard about.

Obviously composting has its rewards — spiritual, as in the case of this very literate man, and earthly, in the form of that rich black humus which can do our gardens so much good. Neither of these benefits, unfortunately, comes without a certain amount of effort. To properly build, water and turn a pile takes a little work. That is what this chapter is about. Fortunately there are some techniques and work-saving devices which can make your job easier. I'll discuss some of them. Moreover, I think that once you understand *why* some of these laborious things are necessary, in terms of what is happening in the composting process, the jobs may seem a little more like fun and a little less like drudgery.

GRINDING, CHOPPING, CHIPPING

Much organic matter can not be composted efficiently in its natural form. A cabbage leaf or a pea vine will rot readily enough, but logs or even brush and sticks will not. Neither will the heavy stems of cabbage or broccoli, squash, tomato or pumpkin vines, corn stalks, wet matted leaves, or old jack-o-lanterns. To make things rot faster, they should be ground up, shredded, chopped or chipped into smaller pieces. You know how a spoonful of sugar granules dissolves so much faster than a sugar lump in a cup of tea because more sugar is directly exposed to the liquid. The same sort of things happens in composting.

The key phrase here is "surface area". Grinding big things into little pieces *increases* surface area. A block of wood, for example, has six sides which can be exposed to the elements. Cut the block in half and suddenly there are twelve sides. Cut both *halves* in half and there are twenty-four surfaces. The total amount of wood is still pretty much the same after just three cuts, but you can imagine how much more paint it would take to cover the twenty-four sides of the smaller pieces than it would have taken to paint the six sides of the original one. The arithmetic is easy. You can figure out for yourself how many surfaces there would be if you were to continue cutting at this rate.

A brush chipper, of course, can cut a fairly large stick into a great many tiny pieces in very short order. Smaller pieces of anything in a compost pile means that there are more places where microorganisms can invade the material. Shredded materials need to be turned much less often because the microbes are well dispersed within the pile, attacking things from all sides.

Chopping things up this way also reduces the *bulk* of organic matter. A pile of wood chips is far more compact than a pile of brush. You can put up to four times as many chopped leaves into a compost container as you could whole ones in the same space. Chopping also bruises, cuts, tears or punctures the tough outer skin of some types of vegetable matter and allows bacteria to get at the inner tissue. If this didn't happen, some things would be very slow to decompose. A kernel of corn, for instance, unless it is well chewed and the outer skin broken, will pass untouched through the human alimentary canal, resisting all of the strong digestive juices and bacteria. A fresh apple in a compost heap will soon become a bad apple, turning brown and soft quite quickly, but unless its outer skin is cut or dented, it will take a long time to rot completely.

Grinding or shredding breaks down the cell walls of plant tissue too. Cellulose, the stuff that cell walls are made of, is hard to break down, so grinding helps here. Moisture will ooze from the microscopic plant cells that are broken, making the material moist. You would see this for yourself if you ran lettuce through a shredder. The result would be a sloppy mess, even though the lettuce was not wet to begin with. This, of course, can have an effect on the moisture content of the compost pile.

Ideally, you should have some control over the fineness or coarseness of the stuff that your chopping device or machine produces. In the same way that green materials chopped too fine will make nothing but a green pulpy mess, *dry* materials ground too fine will blend together when mixed with water to form a paste which can dry and form a barrier that is impervious to water and air. This could happen, for example, with the small particles of sawdust produced by a belt sander. Don't throw fine stuff like this away. Use it in the compost, but be sure that it does not get concentrated in one section of the pile.

The cheapest and simplest chopper-chipper is a machete. Machetes are usually available from army surplus stores for about $4.00. And it should be easy enough to find a stump or old plank to use as a chopping block. But wasn't it Thoreau who said something about the man who chops his own wood? He warms himself twice — once by his own exertion and once by burning the fruits of his labor. It would seem to *me* that any man who used a machete to chop up a whole *lot* of his own garden debris and leaves would be warming himself a lot more than he had to. Still, a lot of people build good compost piles this way. Different folks have different ways of getting their exercise, I guess.

A slightly more expensive alternative might be the four-tined shredding attachment called the Mulch-Away which can be bolted onto the bottom of almost any rotary lawn mower. The Mulch-Away is available from Better Life Enterprises, 1462 John St., Whiting, Indiana 46394. The price is $4.75.

Any rotary lawn mower, by the way, can serve as a pretty good shredder, either with or without a Mulch-Away. Lay whatever it is you want to chop on the ground and run the machine back and forth over it several times. You can even chip up sticks this way. Be sure that you aim the open end or chute toward some sort of backstop such as a wall or a piece of plywood propped against a cart. If you don't, you will have trouble finding and gathering much of the shredded material that is blown out of the mower.

An ordinary kitchen blender, another fairly common household item, is a handy tool for preparing kitchen waste and garbage for composting, as I mentioned earlier. It is a simple matter to keep some sort of a closed container (a large coffee can with a plastic lid works fine for us) on a back corner of the counter top. You can throw all of your compostable garbage into it: rinds and peelings of all kinds, carrot scrappings and tops, pea pods, outer leaves from lettuce and cabbage, egg shells, coffee grounds and tea leaves, even chicken and fish bones. (I know from experience that you can grind up the bones from two entire medium-sized chickens in one blender load.) Leave

out fat, meat scraps and large bones which will stall the machine and are better fed to the family dog anyhow. When the container has accumulated enough stuff, throw some of it in the blender, add a little water and throw the switch. You will be making a beautifully rich garbage soup. Pour this wet slurry onto your pile, spreading it around so that all of it does not wind up in the same spot.

The very best tool for any job, of course, is the one designed to do exactly what the task calls for. There are many "composting machines" on the market these days. These are organic-matter grinders, powered by electric or small gasoline motors. We have tested a lot of these.

Some choppers are a good deal better than others, ranging in price from about $150 to $600. As is usually the case, the better ones have the higher price tags. This is one reason why we keep recommending that several neighbors get together to share the cost of one high-quality machine. The very best ones can easily handle the composting chores for three or four families and still be idle enough of the time to be rented out to other people in the community.

The basic advantage of a compost grinder-shredder is that it both chops the material and *mixes* it. If you feed different materials into the machine at the same time, the end product is a uniform aggregate of the different kinds of organic matter, such as leaves and sticks, dry hay and new grass clippings. It should be powerful enough to accept all kinds of things without stalling out or clogging up: wet rubbery leaves, heavy brush, manure, chunks of hard clay, and stones. Some even have a special feed which will chew up a log as large as three inches in diameter. Anything much bigger than that makes good firewood and probably should not be composted anyway.

If you are considering buying one, shop carefully for your chopper. Choose one compatible with the size of your property (or properties if you decide to go into it on a cooperative basis), your composting ambitions and your garden's needs. Be sure to pick out a machine that is ruggedly built. All choppers are subject to tremendous vibrations, and some fall apart all too quickly.

Electric machines seem to be a good deal less powerful than their gasoline-powered cousins. They have the added disadvantage of requiring electrical outlets and heavy extension cords. "Shredder-baggers" which deposit compost material in neat bags tend to be less expensive, but too underpowered to be *really* good compost shredders. The bags somehow seem like an unnecessary and costly luxury, especially if you are going to use the stuff on the pile right away. Bagging has advantages only if you use your shredder as you would a trash compactor, as a cleaning-up device, and not as a true recycling machine.

Choose a machine that is easy for *you* to move around. You may have to move it more than you think. One chopper we know of has motorized wheels — a beautiful feature. Some grinders are designed to hook onto a small garden tractor and use the tractor as a power source.

Take some time to examine the mechanism that actually shreds the material. Some models have rotary blades similar to those on a lawn mower, others have fixed knives mounted on a horizontal shaft. Some have hammermill-like flails — which is apparently the most efficient system of all. Find out *if* and how well you can regulate the size of the particles in the aggregate you will be making. Most good machines have a series of removable rods, screens or grates which are meant to help you determine the texture of the material that comes out.

Once you have reduced your potential compost to fairly small pieces, either by working it by hand or with the help of some machine, start giving some thought to how wet it should be to be most easily decomposed.

WATERING

The amount of water you have in your compost pile is *fairly* critical, but you have plenty of leeway in which to work and should not get uptight about exact measurements and percentages. It is as simple as this: If the moisture content is much greater than 60%, you run the risk of having an anaerobic pile; if it is much less than 40%, organic matter will not decompose rapidly enough, because the bacteria are deprived of the moisture they need to carry on their metabolism.

The ideal, of course, would be to maintain a constant moisture percentage which is somewhere in this 40-60% range, keeping the water intake exactly equal to the amount of water which is given off to the atmosphere through evaporation. This, as you can imagine, is nearly impossible without laboratory-like conditions. All you should try to do, then, is see that your pile always has the consistency of a "wrung-out sponge."

The microcommunity within the pile, remember, is very sensitive to any changes in its environment. In other words, the moisture content, like the temperature and oxygen supply, dictates what microorganisms will live or die, which will become active and which will remain as inactive spores. If you change the percentage of moisture in the pile you will no doubt be killing some allies. But don't fret. Others will be along shortly to take their places, and they will do just as good a job. On the other hand, anaerobic bacteria are not considered friendly helpers in many composting situations. A pile with *too* much water is likely to have too little oxygen and will give off that unmistakably foul odor which is a sure sign that anaerobes are present.

How do you know when compost is too dry? If you stand next to your pile and find ants "swarming up your legs," as Josephine Neuse

puts it, you can probably assume that your compost lacks some of the moisture it needs. Add water. Ants are symptoms of a too-dry condition.

Your biggest problem, as I see it, will be getting enough moisture to *all* parts of the pile. I have heard it said that the moisture content must be about right if the surface particles in the pile "glisten" with wetness. This is more than a little misleading. Soaking a pile with a garden hose until water runs off it does not necessarily mean that water is sinking through to all of the lower layers. In fact, squirting water on the surface might do no more than moisten the top one inch of material.

Sometimes, if water gets only to its outer layers, a pile will dry out *faster!* The outer surfaces can cake — preventing *both* water and air penetration. If this seems to have happened in your pile, you might try poking some holes for water percolation as well as aeration. Even if you do, when it comes time to turn the pile, you may be disappointed to discover small pockets of dry material where little decay has been going on. In the long run, you may also find that you have to dismantle the pile somewhat and add water here and there if you have a serious drought problem.

The best thing is to moisten the pile as you build it. If it is properly moistened to begin with, it is likely to stay that way. Again, fresh green materials, particularly ones that have been chopped or shredded, should need to have little or no moisture added. Dry hay, sawdust, straw, peat moss or ground corn cobs should be thoroughly moistened before they go into the pile.

If you have the right kind of nozzle on your garden hose, dampen each new layer with a gentle spray. A real blast of water is not too effective and may disrupt the structure of the pile below. If you see water running out of the bottom of the pile, you are over-watering, and are doing little more than leaching out some of the valuable nutrients you are trying so hard to collect.

Rain water is the best kind to put on compost. It picks up lots of oxygen, minerals and microorganisms as it falls through the air. Don't forget that you can "dish" the top of your pile to collect rain water. Unpolluted pond water is good too. Some people throw dish water on their heaps. This may contain some good organic matter, but it also has detergents and grease which may coat some of the vegetable matter, preventing aeration and inhibiting decomposition. Dish water, no. Cooking water, yes! — that is if you are not going to save it for soups, stews, or further cooking.

When all else fails, use good common sense when it comes to watering. Reach part way into the pile in various spots and feel what is going on. If it is warm there, and feels more or less like a squeezed-out sponge, everything is probably in great shape.

TURNING

Turning your pile is the only "bummer" — the only real chore in the whole business of compost making. A cubic yard of finished compost, you will recall, weighs about a ton; compost-in-the-making slightly less. If you are inclined that way, you can figure out beforehand how much weight you are going to have to lift. Leonard Wickenden reminds us, reassuringly, that *without* turning compost at all, nature will take its course just as it always has. This is grist for your mill if you are good at rationalizing about *not* going through the effort of reorganizing your pile. But turning is worth the sweat. It decreases decomposition time. And this is, after all, one of the things composting is all about.

Unfortunately, you can not rely on earthworms and other macroorganisms to do much of your turning for you. Earthworms are great workers. So are ants, mites and other insects. But because worms are weak "pushers", they must literally eat their way through the materials in the pile. They do a lot of good things but cannot bring the "outside of the heap to the inside and the top to the bottom" the way you can with a five or six-tined pitchfork — unless, of course, you have discovered a breed of particularly gifted worms. Inoculating the pile with earthworms in the hope they will do your turning for you, is a waste of time.

In comparison to earthworms, ants are the real muscle men. They can move materials around like mad. But you already know that if your pile has ants, it probably needs water. So worms and bugs can only do a little bit of mixing and reorganizing for you, mostly in the outer perimeters of the heap.

How often you turn your pile depends largely on how ambitious you are. In general, it *should* seem that the more turning you do, the faster rotting will take place. But this is true only to a certain point. As you turn, you *are* mixing well rotted material with fresh, green material with withered matter, wet stuff with dry stuff. All of this speeds decay. If a pile is turned *too* often, on the other hand, microorganisms will not have a chance to get much done. Each time you disturb the pile you are killing a few fungi, actinomycetes and bacteria, and their work is slowed down until they are able to regroup, regrow, and reorganize.

The temperature in your pile might help you decide how often you should turn it. If a pile has a near-perfect carbon-nitrogen ratio (see Chapter 7) and is composed of ground or chopped material, it could reach a temperature peak of 150 degrees Fahrenheit as often as every three or four days. You might want to turn it that often if you are intent on having a thermophilic pile. Normally though, the cycle is longer than that. To keep it at maximum heating capacity, turn the pile whenever your thermometer tells you that the temperature has dropped below 104 degrees Fahrenheit. But using temperature as your sole guide for turning means a lot of careful monitoring and a lot of muscle work for you.

Most casual composters are content to achieve thermophilic temperatures which last for only a few days. This is usually enough time for a satisfactory thermal kill. Later, they allow the pile to cool off as the mesophiles take over and perform their good work. When this happens, pathogenic spores and weed seeds may survive for a while — at least until the pile is turned again and more heat is generated. Many home compost piles can be turned as infrequently as every six weeks to three months, *unless* the compost suddenly seems to be giving off a lot of odor.

If foul odor does become a serious problem, do not panic and cart all of your hard work off to the dump. Begin turning your pile regularly — every day if you can. This will get oxygen into the materials. Ammonia is one of the gases produced when nitrogenous materials are broken down. Another reason for turning the pile then is to permit some of this ammonia to escape.

Layers of bluish-gray mold — which are obviously not actinomycetes — are danger signals. They are another clear indication of an anaerobic condition. Turning and fluffing the organic matter will solve this problem. Smells and molds should soon disappear.

The most efficient way to turn your heap and see that the organic matter gets thoroughly *re*mixed is to cut down the sides of the pile in vertical slices. An ordinary spade works best for this if the ingredients of the pile are not too stringy. If they are, it is best to go back to that old stand-by called the pitchfork. If you are a curious soul, this vertical slicing technique will give you an interesting cross-section view of what things look like inside the pile.

A removable compost container (see illustration) is ideal for this

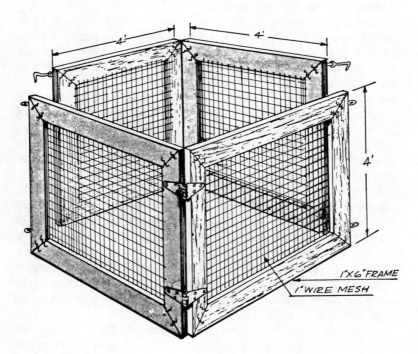

4'   4'

4'

1"x6"FRAME
1"WIRE MESH

turning method. You can dismantile it, set it up again right next to the old pile, and move old material to the new location. Lots of composters who have permanent multi-container systems try to schedule things so that the compost from one full container can be turned into an empty one right next to it. You may find that trying to turn a pile *within* a single container becomes a frustrating sort of haphazard process. You can never be quite sure about what you have turned and what you have not.

Whatever your personal turning, watering or grinding procedure may be, keep a close eye — and a close nose — on the heap. When things do not seem to be working properly there, or if nothing seems to be happening at all, roll up your sleeves and go to work.

7

Things You Might Worry About A Little

A N EXPERT in any field, it seems, is a little like an octopus. You can follow him through familiar waters for just so long and then suddenly — and often unwittingly — he will hide behind an inkscreen of indecipherable statistics, jargon, formulae or other jabberwocky. Sophisticated gardeners and highly technical composting experts are no exception. After a certain point they can become difficult, if not impossible to understand. You and I can become the same if we are not careful.

At first, as a totally inexperienced gardener, I was easily bugged by gardening and composting literature which would throw elementary terms like pH, C/N and NPK at me. I wanted to immediately know *how* to make compost or grow peas. I didn't think I needed complicated explanations as to *why*. Fundamentals seemed like a pain in the neck. "pH" intimidated me most because it reminded me of high school chemistry, which I hated and very nearly failed as a result. "C-N" made me think only of the Canadian National railway system, which I was *sure* had nothing to do with compost. I found "NPK" annoying because for the longest time I could not remember whether the P stood for phosphorous or whether the P stood for potassium. (Whoever assigned "K" as the symbol for potassium, anyway?) I know that many other new gardeners have shared my frustration.

The temptation in situations like these is to write off the things we do not understand, categorizing them as "unimportant." It is easy to shrug and say, "I won't worry about it," when in fact, what you are being told *is* important and is something you *should* worry about. For example, if you know nothing else about your garden soil, you should know its pH. Plants will literally be poisoned if the pH is much too high or low. The pH of the compost you put into the garden will have a marked effect on the soil there. Hence, it is a good idea to have some understanding of what pH is all about.

pH, C/N and NPK can all be explained in reasonably simple terms. They are much simpler than, say, some of the microbiological complexities we have already covered. If you are an experienced gardener and already know a great deal about these things, skip this chapter entirely, or regard it as helpful review. For the rest of us: It is as much a mistake not to understand as it is for the experts to assume that we *do*.

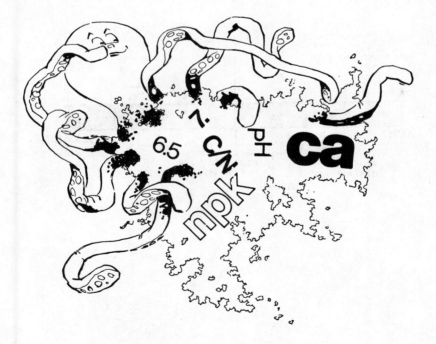

pH

The term pH, as you may or may *not* recall from school chemistry, describes the *alkalinity* ("sweetness") or *acidity* ("sourness") of soil, compost or some other substance. pH is usually expressed as a number. The pH scale runs from 1, indicating pure acidity, to 14, —

The pH Scale and some commonly known substances

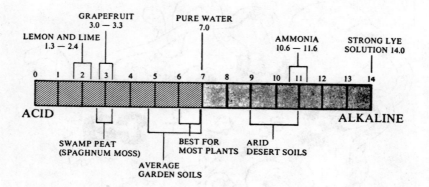

purely alkaline, or "basic" as it is sometimes called. Something neutral would be described as 7, halfway between 1 and 14. The neutral zone, somewhere around 7, is desirable for most plants. Most bacteria and fungi operate best in a medium with pH from 6.5 to slightly over 7. Clearly then, you want to keep your compost pile within this range.

To lime or not to lime; that is the question. Lime or crushed limestone raises the pH, neutralizing acidic compost or making basic compost *more* alkaline. Ground clam shells, crushed oyster shells, wood ashes, Dolomite, bone meal and marl (a limey clay taken from stream beds) are some of the other things that operate the same way and are frequently called lime substitutes.

When manure and oak leaf mold are mixed in with other organic matter, they will generally lower the pH of compost. Gypsum (calcium sulphate) and alum (aluminum sulphate) will neutralize alkaline soil or compost far more quickly than these organic substances, but they should be used prudently.

You can find out just how "sweet" or just how "sour" your compost is by having it analyzed. Send a sample to your State University Extension Service just the way you would send a soil sample, or to a private laboratory such as Prescription Soil Analysis, Lincoln, Nebraska, 68501 or to Garden Way Laboratories, Charlotte, Vt., 05445.

You can also test it yourself. There are a number of good, inexpensive home soil test kits that you can buy. One is the Fisher Alkacid Soil Tester put out by the Fisher Scientific Company, Fair Lawn, New Jersey 07410. This consists of test ribbon — which comes in plastic containers like small Scotch-Tape dispensers — and a color chart. The idea is to take a representative sample of your compost by gathering bits from various parts of the heap, and mixing them together as well as you can. Then, you dilute about a thimble-full of this mixture in distilled water. (Distilled water is put into automobile batteries. Any service station should have it.) You dip a piece of the test ribbon into this muddy mixture, and the ribbon will change color. By comparing the color of the tape to the color chart, you will get a fairly accurate reading of your compost's pH.

The Sudbury Soil Test Kit from Sudbury Laboratories, Sudbury, Mass. 01776 can give you a nitrogen-phosphorous-potassium (NPK) analysis as well as an acidity test. Here you must mix a compost sample with various chemical fluids in a small test tube. The fluids and test tubes are all provided. You compare the color of the mixture against another very simple color chart. Testing your own compost may be easier than you think. No home composter, by the way, should have to spend more than $8 to $10 for such a testing kit.

Tests like these are certainly not a bad idea. You *should* try to keep yourself informed about the goings-on in your compost heap. Keep in mind, though, that in many cases it may not be necessary to worry about controlling a pile's pH at all. Decaying compost will naturally go through a normal pH cycle. In the earliest stages of decomposition the material tends to become acidic. If you were to do a pH test only a couple of weeks áfter activating the pile, you might get a very distorted reading.

Later on, a healthy pile will neutralize itself on its own, as long as it is getting enough oxygen. As a matter of fact, it is probably safe to say that building and maintaining an aerobic pile which is made up of a wide variety of organic matter will almost automatically result in compost with a pH very close to 7. In other words, do not assume that your pile is going to be very acidic and start adding lime or some sort of lime substitute, unless the major portion of the pile is composed of some highly acidic materials such as oak leaves, pine needles or pine sawdust.

Unnecessary liming can be dangerous. In a pile that is already functioning well, it may do more harm than good by promoting the loss of nitrogen in the form of ammonia. (An ammonia smell, incidentally, immediately tells you that the pH is too high.) If a pile is too "sweet" because of over-liming; bacteria and other microorganisms are threatened. At very best, they will not be functioning at optimum efficiency. Microbes are happiest in an environment that is *slightly* acidic — just under 7.

If the materials in your pile *are* very acidic or, for some reason, there is poor aeration within the pile, you can probably benefit from lime. Anaerobic bacteria produce lots of organic acids, and an alkaline substance such as lime will counteract their effect. Lime or ground limestone have the added advantage of contributing calcium, an important element for plants. They will also diminish nasty odors which sometimes emanate from dead animals or animal matter in the heap.

Old wives' tales in many places have it that lime placed next to animal manure will rob the manure of all its nitrogen. Sir Albert Howard and other experimenters including some at the University of

Vermont, have proven this *not* to be the case; although it may be so with so-called "quicklime." Quicklime (calcium oxide) is freshly-burned lime. It is caustic and can literally destroy good humus. This is why it reacts so poorly with manure. Gardeners almost never use quicklime today, and besides, there is very little of it around. So don't worry about using lime and manure together.

This section in a nutshell: be conscious of your pile's pH. If simple tests, taken after the pile has been working for several weeks, show a high level of either acidity or alkalinity, cope with it by neutralizing the pile with one or more of the things mentioned above.

C/N

The C/N, another often mystifying abbreviation, expresses the relationship between carbonaceous materials (C) and nitrogenous matter (N) in your compost system. This important relationship is stated in the form of a ratio. For instance, humus usually has a C/N of around 10:1, ten parts of carbon to one part of available nitrogen. The first number always tells you the parts of carbon as compared to *one* part of nitrogen — 10:1, 25:1, 40:1, 154:1, and so on. To simplify things, compost scientists and other people who discuss the C/N frequently leave off the "to one" (:1) part of the ratio, stating the C/N as a single number — 10, 25, 40, or 154.

Here are some average C/N's for a few compostable materials that are often used:

grass clippings	25
oak leaves	50
manure with bedding	23
sawdust	150-500
straw, cornstalks and cobs	50-100
vegetable trimmings	25
leguminous plants (peas, beans, soybeans)	15
animal droppings	15
pine needles	60-110
alder or ash leaves	25

Some people say that getting the right carbon-nitrogen ratio in your compost is similar to mixing a very dry martini. This is not really an apt analogy because the lesser ingredient in the compost, the nitrogen, is far more important than the lesser ingredient in the cocktail, vermouth. The ideal C/N for effective composting is around 25. A pile having a C/N a great deal higher than that will take forever, figuratively speaking, for the material to be broken down. This is why a pile of oak leaves or a mound of sawdust and wood chips will sit for years without much apparent decay.

But the C/N need not be exact. You will probably have no precise way of measuring it anyway. Just remember: When you use materials like straw (150-500), ground corn cobs (50-100) or sawdust (150-500), the bacteria in your pile are going to need some help. Add nitrogen in some form.

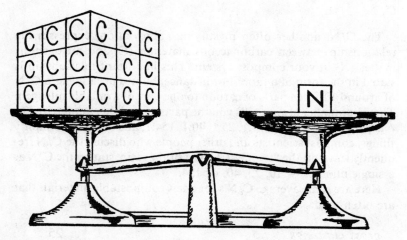

How much? By adding *too* much nitrogenous material, you are manufacturing ammonia, and nitrogen, one of the components in ammonia, is given off and wasted. Adding two to three pounds of some nitrogen supplement, such as manure, bloodmeal, cottonseed meal or loam, for every one hundred pounds of highly carbonaceous raw material, will usually bring the ratio down to within a reasonable range. Green material will require far less, because it is high in nitrogen already.

In order to be on the safe side and to keep the C/N from getting too fouled up, try keeping a small surplus of nitrogen in the pile, even if this means a loss of some nitrogen as a *little* ammonia escapes from the material. Most of this discussion becomes academic when you realize that, by putting "activator" in your pile, you have already provided nitrogen supplement and have already adjusted the C/N without giving it much thought.

Once you have understood what C/N is all about, you can recognize when something is out of whack and take steps to correct it. If the decomposition in your pile seems too slow, and the pile surely does not need watering or turning, reduce the C/N by adding more activator. If the strong scent of ammonia comes wafting out of the pile, you know that you have added too much. In that case, turn the pile or leave it alone for a while. The excess of nitrogen should correct itself, as some of it drifts off into the atmosphere. If this is *not* the case, check the pH after a week or so. Maybe *it* is too high.

The nitrogen content in a compost pile, like the pH, goes through a natural cycle. In the earliest stage nitrogen is expended. The bacteria consume it voraciously as they frantically multiply to cope with the new material. This is the time when the pile needs nitrogen supplement the most.

Next, assuming that the C/N is somewhere between 15 and 30, the nitrogen content of the pile is more or less stabilized as the bacteria make usable nitrogen at approximately the same rate as they use it up. In the third stage, the nitrogen level starts to build up as some of the microorganisms die and decompose themselves, thereby contributing nitrogen to the compost.

Finished compost will probably not have a C/N as low as that of humus. If it is between 14 and 20, it should be satisfactory for most purposes. Have you been following this discussion closely enough to realize that finished compost has nearly the same C/N as animal droppings. That's the whole point. The reason for making compost to begin with is to produce synthetic manure.

NPK

NPK, as you probably realize by now, describes the content of the *major nutrients* necessary for plant life and growth — nitrogen, phosphorous and potassium. Minor or *secondary nutrients* include calcium (Ca), magnesium (Mg) and iron (Fe). Plants need a total of sixteen nutrients, some in very tiny quantities. These are called *trace elements,* including zinc, boron, cobalt, molybdenum, copper and manganese, to name just a few.

The numbers on a package of commercial fertilizer tell you the

NPK content of the chemical inside. If the package says "10-6-4," this means that the fertilizer contains 10% nitrogen, 6% phosphorous, and 4% potassium. Different types of fertilizers contain different NPK's. 10-6-4 or 20-10-5 are called "complete fertilizers" because they contain a certain percentage of all three major nutrients. Superphosphate (0-20-0) on the other hand, is "incomplete" because it only contains a percentage of phosphorous, and no significant percentage of either nitrogen or potassium.

It may seem that we have belabored the various ways of getting nitrogen into your compost. But try never to underestimate the importance of nitrogen. It is perhaps the most important nutrient of all, mainly because plants themselves contain so much of it. It gives them their healthy dark green color and is essential for leaf and stem growth. You will easily recognize a plant with nitrogen deficiency by its sickly yellow coloring. The problem with nitrogen is that it is so "mobile." That means that it escapes from compost or soil very easily, either in the form of gas or by being washed away. One of the most important reasons for composting at all is to restore nitrogen to the soil. So obviously you should be making as much effort as possible to store up nitrogen in your compost pile.

Phosphorous stimulates growth, flowering and root development in plants. Cell division is vital to plant growth; and it would be impossible without the presence of phosphorous. Plants without phosphorous grow slowly, if at all, look droopy, and have weak root systems. But phosphorous, very much unlike nitrogen, is "immobile". It tends to stay for a long time wherever it is applied. It does not leach and is not given off as a gas.

Years ago farmers in some parts of Vermont recognized the lack of phosphorous in their soil and began spreading superphosphate on their fields. Today as a result of their diligence, much of the soil in the state has too much phosphorous. *You* may not want to add superphosphate to your compost pile unless there is a definite phosphorous deficiency in your garden or unless you are preparing some kind of specialized potting compound.

Potassium is necessary for the development of chlorophyll, that almost-magical substance in green plants that makes the miracle of photosynthesis possible. Potassium also strengthens plant tissue and makes vegetation more disease resistant. Plants which receive too little "potash" look stunted. Potassium (or potash) washes out of compost quite easily, but it can never escape as a gas. You can restore it to the heap or to the garden by adding wood ashes or muriate of potash.

Many composter-gardeners worry too much about producing compost with a very high and well balanced NPK. Would it be terribly disillusioning to be told that compost is *not* a miracle fertilizer — in spite of what some proponents of purely organic gardening would have us believe? In most excellent compost the content of NPK is actually very low. In fact, it usually does not have a high enough percentage of NPK to be considered a fertilizer at all. Only when it is supplemented with something like 10-6-4 can it be considered a complete fertilizer.

People who are bent on balancing the NPK in their compost piles are missing the point. Compost's immeasurable value extends far beyond contributing major nutrients to the garden. It releases what nutrients it has — or what nutrients you have given it — *gradually,* not all in one shot as will an application of chemicals. It withholds some of its "goodies", making nutrients available to plants for a longer period of time.

Don't misjudge the quality of your compost on the sole basis of its NPK. *That* can always be adjusted. Remember that humus is, after all, a happy composite of organic matter and many different minerals. Trace elements are important too. A compost which has been created out of many different things is likely to be rich in them. The *most* important gift you present to your garden through compost is an addition to the soil life. Compost might best be judged according to the amount of microbial life it has. The basic questions are: What kinds of microorganisms are there? How well *have* they done their jobs in the compost pile? And, how *will* they perform in the garden?

HEATING

I have already mentioned the practice of using temperature as a factor in helping you determine when to turn the pile. Some gardeners are *reluctant* to turn their heaps, because they are afraid it is going to lose a lot of its heat. They are right, of course. But the pile will regenerate heat again very quickly, sometimes in a matter of two to twelve hours. In other words, turning interrupts the heat fermentation process only briefly.

Composters seem to worry about heating more than anything else. A friend of mine, a new gardener, came out of his door one chilly morning and was horrified to discover steamy vapor rising out of the ventilation holes in his pile. He nervously mentioned it to several of us over lunch. When he was finally assured that vapor was not cause for alarm and that it was, in fact, reason to cheer, others in the group immediately began to express concern that their piles did *not* give off a lot of steam.

Generally, I think we have placed too much emphasis and value on *home* compost pile temperatures which are as high as 150 or 160 degrees Fahrenheit. Sanitation in massive public compost systems is one thing, but it is not necessarily true that higher temperatures mean faster decomposition. Thermophilic composting does have the advantage of killing pathogenic organisms and weed seeds. Mesophiles do not perform this function, but these mid-temperature bacteria are every bit as effective "rotters" as thermophiles. If you don't use plant refuse, hay or straw that has gone to seed, and if you don't use diseased matter, you should not have to worry about *intense* heating all that much.

You want *some* heat. Psychrophiles will be at work even at very low temperatures, but for decomposition to be at all effective, the temperature of the pile must be above 55 degrees. On the other hand, heating can be tricky if it gets out of hand. Earthworms are killed at 130 degrees Fahrenheit, and they will not stick around and endanger themselves for very long in temperatures that even approach that figure. Excessive heat is far more dangerous than no heat at all. Azobacteria, the precious microorganisms that transform nitrogen gas into a form that plants can use, are killed at temperatures above 160. So try to establish some sort of a happy medium as far as heat is concerned.

A non-thermal way of killing weed seeds in compost, by the way, was developed at the University of Rhode Island. It is apparently a good alternative if you do not get your pile to heat up enough and do not mind mixing chemicals. Cyanamid (calcium cyanamide) added at a rate of 13 pounds per cubic yard of organic matter will destroy weed seeds in four to six weeks. It is important that the Cyanamid (a commercial name) be thoroughly mixed with the compost.

A pile that is too small may give off a lot of its heat to the surrounding atmosphere. This may account for its apparent lack of heating. But the inability to accumulate enough materials for a big pile should not be an excuse for not composting at all. Do not be discouraged and start thinking that you cannot make good compost because a lot of heat does not build up in your pile. If your pile is activated with soil for instance, don't expect it to heat up as much as a neighboring one that is activated with manure.

Compost piles work most efficiently in the summer months, because the surrounding air is warmer, and slower during the rest of the year. In fall, winter and early spring the heating-up process can be enhanced and the pile made to function longer if you insulate it and add lots of high-nitrogen materials like leguminous plants and animal matter. Whenever you do this, of course, you lower the carbon-nitrogen ratio and should expect to sacrifice some nitrogen in exchange for this extra heat.

You need no fancy and costly devices to gauge and record the temperature near the middle of the pile, nor a calculator to understand the NPK or the C/N, and no elaborate testing equipment to know the pH. If you have no telethermometer, stick a piece of metal pipe into the pile and leave it there for a few minutes. If you then pull out the pipe and it feels hot or warm, all is probably well.

By far the most frequently asked question about compost making is, "How long does it take?" That will be answered later. But the second most popular question has to be "Why won't my pile heat up?" Your neighbor may ask you this. And suddenly *you* are the compost expert — the sophisticated gardener. The question is complex, one which this book has been answering, directly or indirectly, since the outset.

Don't throw an octopus's inkscreen at your neighbor, now that you know some fundamentals. Explain to him that failure to heat may have to do with things like a poor mixture of the organic materials, with the moisture content, with the amount and kind of activator that was used, with the C/N, with the pH, with the fact that the pile needs turning, with the fact that it is just too cold outside, or possibly even with the fact that the compost is more or less finished — rotted all it is going to rot for the time being.

Many of these possibilities, like so many of the many of life's little complexities, are inextricably interrelated. By now you should have a pretty good rudimentary knowledge of composting microbiology, of theory, mechanics, and even a smattering of gardening philosophy. You are qualified to make a diagnosis. Encourage your neighbor to experiment a little if, together, you suspect that his lack of heat might result from something like the C/N being a bit out of kilter. Above all, assure him that he *can do no harm* by trying different things.

Finally, after all your patient and helpful explanations are complete, don't be surprised if you end up sharing my wife's experience of not so many years ago. Our young daughter expressed concern about and interest in reading. Several days were spent teaching her to recite the twenty-six letters of the alphabet — the very rudiments of written language. When she finally had learned it all, she said, "Yes Mommy, but how do I *read?*"

8

Famous Concoctions and Alternate Approaches

Now that some groundwork has been laid, in the form of basic composting fundamentals, let's have a look at some well-publicized recipes and at some of the other composting possibilities that are open to you. But don't try to use any one of these descriptions as a definitive model. A smart composter, like a good cook or an experienced carpenter, adapts recipes or blueprints to fit his or her needs and materials. Compromise. Take something from each if you can. There is no known law that says you cannot be composting several different ways at the same time.

THE INDORE PROCESS

In a book called *Soil and Health: A Study of Organic Agriculture* published in 1947, England's Sir Albert Howard defined the composting process in fairly concise terms:

> [It is] . . . the collection and admixture of vegetable and animal wastes off of the area farmed into heaps or pits, kept at a degree of moisture resembling that of a squeezed-out sponge, turned, and emerging at the end of three months as a rich, crumbling compost, containing a wealth of plant nutrients and organics essential for growth.

Howard was concerned about what he called the "waste products of agriculture", which he saw as too valuable to simply throw away. In this sense, by making a real effort to find something truly beneficial to do with them, he was a man far ahead of his time, a forerunner of the organic-conservationist-ecology movement which was still waiting in the wings.

A reading of Sir Albert's complex descriptions of his Indore composting procedures would impress you with the exactitude of his scientific investigations. You might also get the distinct impression, I am sorry to say, that if you did not follow his instructions to the letter, nothing in the way of decomposition would happen in your compost pile.

This, as you have been assured so *many* times before, is nonsense. Rotting is rotting. Working microorganisms haven't the slightest notion whether they exist in some scientifically-conceived compost system or whether they are in fact in some lonely and forgotten corner of someone's woodlot — just as plants have no way of distinguishing between nutrients that are fed to them organically and those that are provided more directly through chemicals.

Today, several generations after his original writings were published, it is easy to belittle and criticize Howard's work. Let us not forget, however, that his efforts were those of a pioneer in, what for most of western civilization, at least, was a nearly forgotten field. Let's remember too that his extremely specific and precise directions for making compost were especially suited for a particular set of physical and climatic conditions in Indore, India where the early experiments were performed. It would be silly for you, me, or anyone else to follow his dictates religiously, because it is very unlikely that circumstances where we live exactly match those of Indore. His rules may not work quite as well, in fact, anywhere else.

In spite of his apparent inflexibility, Sir Albert Howard's composting methods were based on four valid principles, all of which are still applicable:

(1) The building of compost piles in *sandwich-like layers* to encourage the alternation of green or wet materials with dry withered matter.

(2) The necessity of *accurate moisture content* within the pile, in order for the microbial life to operate efficiently.

(3) *Optimum pile size,* taking into consideration the problems of compaction, heating and insulation.

(4) Ultimately *good aeration,* which allows the growth of aerobic bacteria, as one of the requirements for good decomposition.

In the actual Indore process, Howard was composting on a much larger scale than he later recommended for the New Zealand box, which he saw as a convenient size container for the home gardener. His *original* piles and pits — which were anaerobic in most cases — held a much greater volume of materials that the New Zealand box would have. He recommended an "admixture" of wastes that consisted of two thirds vegetable matter, one third manure, and an amount of activator which was to equal 1% of the vegetable waste.

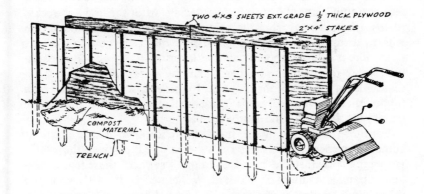

AN ALTERNATIVE COMPOSTING SYSTEM — *much like a mini-trench silo — modeled after the open concrete areas used for storing silage on large livestock farms.*

This is a good way to get around having to turn your compost by hand, and a great way to put your rotary tiller to good use at times when you are not able to use it in the garden.

The distance between the plywood sidewalls should be just a little greater than the width of the tiller. Pile organic matter in the open-ended container — making the pile highest in the center and tapering it gradually toward either end. As you drive your machine through, the tines should mix and turn the material for you.

An Indore-type pile can be built by laying down alternate six inch layers of green and dry vegetable matter, two inches of manure on top of that, and then a sprinkling of dried blood, hoof, horn meal or soil. Once this is done, complete the same layering process again. Water the heap until it has the consistency of a squeezed-out sponge. Then poke ventilation holes in the pile with a long crowbar. These holes should reach right down to the earth at the bottom of the pile.

For the first six weeks after the pile has been started, the composter should heed two danger signals: (1) A bad odor with the presence of flies, meaning that the pile has been over-watered, and (2) "arrested fermentation" caused by too *little* watering. After the first six weeks, remove the material from the original pile and build a second one with it, turning and remixing the organic matter as you do so. This time there is no need to worry about layering. Allow the compost in pile No. 2 to ripen as you begin making a new pile out of fresh materials on the site of the first one. By the end of another six weeks (about three months all told), the batch of compost in pile No. 2 should be "finished" and ready for use.

For those of us like you and me who already know a *little* bit about compost science, there is nothing new here really. Since the 1940's gardening specialists have improved upon some of these techniques and expanded some of Sir Albert's principles. In the 1930's, on the other hand, his ideas might have seemed revolutionary. We can thank him directly for much of what we now know about modern composting.

THE UNIVERSITY OF CALIFORNIA METHOD

It strikes me as somehow significant that it has been Americans, specifically, compost scientists at the University of California, who have worked out a way to make "quick" compost. We seem to be infatuated with instantaneousness. We are programmed to expect and *enjoy* instant coffee, instant pudding, instant breakfast, instant iced tea, "instant" anything, even micro-wave ovens that will cook a roast in "practically a jiffy." I hear that people with newer sets don't need to suffer the frustration of having to wait that few seconds for the television to warm up. Now there is instant T.V. reception.

If you are just starting a garden and feel you need compost "right now," I would say that the University of California method is more than worth the effort. With it you can make "usable" compost in fourteen days. Three things are necessary for its success:

(1) *Chopping or shredding* is important because it will increase the surface area of the organic materials.

(2) There must be an *intimate blending* of microorganisms, a nitrogenous activator like manure, carbonaceous materials such as leaves and grass clippings, and vitamins. This is easy enough to accomplish if you mix your raw materials together as they are fed into the shredder. Blending this way will assure a more rapid attack on the part of the microbes.

(3) *Frequent turning* is vital. It should be done every three days at least.

One Saturday morning last October I started a new compost pile by following, more or less, the principles of the University of California method. The pile was to consist of leaves of all kinds, already rotting sticks from the woods surrounding my house, and seedy first cut hay which I brought home in bales.

Everything was chopped before it went into the heap, and was pretty thoroughly mixed. First, a big handful of hay was fed into the shredder, then a handful of leaves, a handful of old dead sticks, and so on. The pile measured about five feet by four feet. Whenever it built up three or four inches, it was given a generous sprinkling of alfalfa meal and was heavily dampened with water from the garden hose. Every eighteen inches or so a thick layer of coarse unchopped hay was added, just to provide clear air channels into the pile.

By mid-afternoon the pile was about five feet high. I told my wife, who was helping me between sprints to rescue children from one another and to reprimand the dog for various indiscretions, that I was going to quit and watch the World Series on television. Actually, I quit because the machine just seemed to keep droning on . . . . . efficiently and indiscriminately grinding up everything I fed it; and I was generally getting bored with the whole job.

After dinner, I returned to close off the open side of the wire-fence compost enclosure by stacking several extra bales of hay there. Then I broke one or two more bales, so that I could put a thick layer of tightly packed "books" or "flakes" of hay on top of the pile for insulation. I then wet down the whole pile one more time for good measure.

By Sunday morning, the compost pile was already warm. In less than a day, the bacteria already in the compost material had decided among themselves who was going to take over and do most of the initial work. They had become so enthusiastic about their project that they were already producing a lot of heat. By Sunday night, the pile was *hot*. On Monday morning, there was a heavy frost, but the pile exuded steamy vapors. Before dinner that evening — two days after it was built — it was clear to me that the heap had already shrunk. The temperature was too high for me to comfortably put my hand beneath the top layers of hay.

Tuesday evening the pile was turned for the first time. And it was turned again every three days after that. On the third Saturday, exactly two weeks after it was made, the pile had cooled down. It was torn apart, loaded into the garden cart, hauled away to the garden in several trips, and spread there. It was certainly a far cry from the dark "crumbling compost" that Sir Albert Howard described, but it had obviously been through partial sterilization as a result of the heat. It was riddled with actinomycetes, the weed seeds had apparently been killed (few of them germinated in the spring anyway), and, in spite of its stringiness caused by the unchopped hay, it smelled rich, earthy and fertile.

By late spring its final decomposition in the garden proper was complete. The soil revealed no evidence of any of the particles of organic matter in the compost, including the wood chips from the old sticks — even though the garden had been through a cold winter with very very little snow-cover protection. Not a bad testimonial for the University of California method, I would say.

Still, I am a little skeptical about some of the published claims I read about concerning high-speed composting. Composting, by definition, necessitates giving Mother Nature a prodding, encouraging her to go about her business a little faster. But as several recognized composting experts have said, you can rot something no faster than the genetics of the microorganisms will permit. Prodding and disturbing *them* too much may only disrupt their labor and interfere with their reproductive processes and subsequent multiplication. I'll bet my fourteen-day compost would have been better still, had it been allowed to ferment longer. The bacteria would have had time to release more nutrients.

And I can't help but wonder if the quality of our lives doesn't suffer some from our overindulgence in instant gratification. As many of us are discovering, "Fastest ain't always bestest." I strongly suspect that this is also the case with compost making.

THE OGDEN-THREE-PILE SYSTEM

If professors at the University of California tell the short of it, Samuel Ogden, Vermont's well known sage, author and organic gardening guru, is their antithesis. He takes the long route. It takes nearly two years of decomposition to "complete" his compost.

Sam Ogden's method has been made famous by his own book, *Step-by Step to Organic Vegetable Gardening*, as well as by others who have written about it. He uses three piles. Each year he removes finished compost from one, and builds another, while the third pile just sits there rotting, undisturbed. Each pile is within a cinder block retaining wall in a space measuring five feet by twelve feet. The fallow pile stands about four and a half feet high.

Mr. Ogden is accustomed to curious daytime visitors like me at his picturesque home in Landgrove — although he is unhappy to have them arrive without calling first. He sells fresh vegetables to several gourmet restaurants in the area, and to other locals who place orders in advance. His vegetables are picked to order each day, just before the customer arrives to pick them up.

When I visited there last, a distinguished-looking gentleman from Washington D.C. was hard at work in the garden setting poles for Romano pole beans — one of Mr. Ogden's favorites. While I was watching him, he was sharply criticized by his white-haired host for not setting the poles exactly straight and plumb. Later when I had a chance to ask the tired guest if he didn't resent that kind of verbal abuse he laughed and said, "I visit here not so much to work Sam's garden as to let him cultivate and discipline my mind."

There can be no mistake on the part of a guest at Ogden's who, late in the evening after good dining, good drink and good talk, finds himself wandering sleepily into the back yard to empty the night's accumulated garbage. It is perfectly clear to anyone, including neighbors who contribute to it, which pile is the one under construction. There is a large hand printed sign stuck in its top that reads, "Put Garbage Here." Whoever follows these directions is expected to cover the garbage with a thin layer of soil to discourage birds and keep out maurading neighborhood dogs.

As the Landgrove summer plays out its brief role, pea vines, weeds, cabbage leaves and other garden residues are added to the compost pile, along with topsoil and a rare application of manure. Mr. Ogden tries to keep the layers thin to allow the free passage of oxygen and carbon dioxide to and from the compost. Oddly enough, he makes a point of keeping leaves and grass clippings out of his piles — even though these are basic staples in many people's compost. Hardwood leaves are too tough and long-lasting, he says, and clippings get hot and slimy. These things, along with other decay-resistant items like corn stalks, should be chopped and stacked separately, he feels, or better still, tilled directly into the garden.

He describes his personal composting style as "the lazy man's method." He does no turning, allows rainfall to take care of all his watering chores, and uses no activators other than leftover manure and soil. In the late fall he covers the newest pile with sod for insulation — root side up, turf side down.

Sir Albert Howard would have undoubtedly considered Samuel Ogden's composting practices highly unscientific. They are. He refuses to worry about things like C/N, pH or the numbers on the sides of bags of fertilizer — which he doesn't buy anyway. Nevertheless his finished product has an amazingly crumbly, almost granular consistency, not unlike the stuff that Howard made. Soil and compost experts would describe it as "colloidal", meaning that it is a homogenous concoction made up of fine particles which are all pretty much the same size.

It is so beautiful in this respect that his friend, critic and fellow author, Catherine Osgood Foster *(The Organic Gardener)* has accused him — in a friendly way — of sifting it through some kind of a screen before letting anyone see it. This he vehemently denies.

His compost, as he showed me, has a lovely sweet smell. It *tastes* sweet too, as he also demonstrated. To that fact I can not truly testify. I was able to persuade him to let me forego that particular test, and must take him at his word. He regards his compost as too scarce and too good to broadcast over his entire garden, so he uses it only under hills and rows, just before planting.

Ogden's reason for composting at all is hardly unique, as he explains in *Step-by Step to Organic Vegetable Gardening*. There is no better "food for the garden," he says, "than well-rotted stable manure." In this day and age, unfortunately, few of us have an unlimited supply of this, and we have to resort to composting. He writes,

> The difference between manure and compost is simple: in the first instance an animal feeds on vegetation and passes the material through his body, extracting nourishment in the process. Thus the waste consists of organic material that has been fragmented and treated with body juices, then subjected to further decomposition due to the complicated action of oxygen and bacteria while the manure is stacked in piles. Compost is, in general, made the same way, with the exception that one step in the process is omitted, that of passing through the body of some animal. The end products are highly similar and, for our purposes, nearly identical . . . A compost pile is a sensible and even necessary adjunct to a garden, for it means the conservation of waste and a reduction in the expense of operation.

MINI-COMPOSTING SYSTEMS

If you live on a small plot of land — or on no land at all — you share a problem with millions of others. You and your family seem to produce a *certain* amount of organic waste, but you never seem to be able to scrounge up enough material to make a respectable-looking compost heap. There is no reason to feel cheated or to cop out on composting altogether. There are some easy composting alternatives that do not involve building large piles that heat up quickly and sustain high temperatures.

Earthworms — with a little help from you when it comes to some of the heavy work — will do a great job of making compost in a small pile that is only a foot and a half or two feet high. The succulent organic matter you put there will invite them from the ground below. You can even·buy earthworms through the mail if you like, and add them to your modest collection of grass clippings, leaves and vegetable wastes.

Mail order worms should not be confused with the kind of worms you might dig or buy on the roadside for use as fishing bait. They are usually "compost worms" that have been bred and raised in the same sort of deliciously-rich surroundings that your mini-pile will offer. Earthworms that sport impressive names like *Red Wiggler, Red Hybrid,* or *California Red,* tend to be spoiled rotten, if you will excuse the expression. They have been so pampered and well fed that they will thrive *only* in compost and will probably do poorly in common every-day garden soil. To buy "reds" or "blue-gray thins" look for advertisements for earthworm companies in gardening magazines like *Horticulture* or *Organic Gardening.* Once you have introduced a few earthworms into your pile, these "intenstines of the soil", as they are sometimes called, will double their numbers in about a month's time.

Just outside the Garden Way Meeting House in Charlotte where different groups of friends, associates, and business acquaintances met almost every day for lunch, we had a small wire cage that was about eighteen inches square and three feet high, in which we made garbage compost. Fresh garbage was put in the top each day, mixed with a few dry leaves if it contained something particularly wet or gooey and sprinkled with alfalfa meal from a container that we kept close at hand. This whole ritual took only a moment longer than dumping it into a garbage can or down a kitchen sink disposer, and getting rid of large quantities of garbage that way meant less frequent trips to the Charlotte dump, which, for some inconvenient reason, was open only on Wednesdays and Saturdays.

Natural layering in our mini-composting device developed as more material was put in, and the pile shrunk quickly, making room for more garbage. We rarely bothered to turn it, if at all, and never seemed to need to add water. The end result after a couple of months of decay was always magnificent compost — alive with earthworms. We used it mostly in the greenhouse as part of a mixture for starting seedlings, or in the garden under newly transplanted tomatoes or beneath squash hills. The plants and the worms seemed to love it. And so did we.

PIT AND TRENCH COMPOSTING

Burying garbage is a good way of killing several birds with one stone. You temporarily dispose of waste materials, eliminate any chance of odor, and can still make use of the fermented residue. Pit composting has the obvious advantage of putting everything out of sight, and for a while at least, out of mind. It also permits the composting material to stay warmer in winter and more damp in summer. The *dis*advantage is that in underground composting you necessarily bring anaerobic bacteria into the act — along with the earthworms whose gizzards will be grinding away at the subterranean garbage.

On the farm, where pit composting is sometimes done on a fairly large scale, underground rotting allows bacteria, anaerobic fungus and worms to transmute stinky masses of manure, urine and litter into sweet smelling soil. At home, if you throw debris into a hole that is twelve or fourteen inches deep and cover it again with loose soil, it will decompose quite quickly. Once the garbage is sufficiently rotted you can do one of two things. You can dig up the compost again and use it somewhere else, or you can plant a shrub, fruit tree, grape vine or berry bush right over the pit.

Some folks with small gardens that are spaded and worked by hand, bury garbage in long trenches. This is a very good idea of course. Vegetable plantings can eventually be made directly on top of the covered trench. But it is not a healthy plan to do this too soon after the trench has been filled. It is better to allow the garbage plenty of time to decompose. Growing food in too-raw garbage can cause stomach problems in humans. Root crops like beets, parsnips, rutabagas and carrots may pick up some unpleasant parasites, which have not yet been destroyed by microbial activities, and then install them in your intestinal tract.

The best trenching method involves a plan which I have heard called "vertical composting." You lay out your garden in three-foot wide rows, dividing each row into three one-foot lanes. If you have doubts about your memory's ability to serve you well, keep records of what you have done each year in each one-foot lane.

Year one: Dig a spade-width trench along the left hand side of each three-foot row. Leave the middle foot as a walkway — a narrow strip of mulch would not hurt here — and make plantings along the right-hand side of the section.

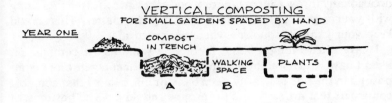

Year two: Use the left-hand side as a walking space. Plant down the middle lane and trench-compost down the right side.

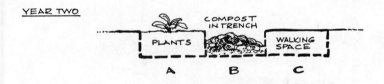

Year three: Trench-compost in the center, walk on the right and plant on the left where the underground garbage, buried during year one, has had a couple of full gardening seasons to rot.

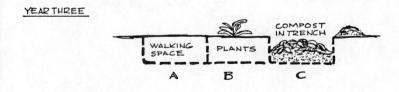

Year four: Repeat what you did during year one.

This is a simple yet systematic soil improvement program which permits you to bury your garbage right in the garden and still keep your stomach in good working order. There is no reason you can not occasionally throw a bit of lime or wood ashes into the trenches along with your vegetable scraps and other organic matter. This should keep your garden's soil somewhere near neutral.

I have often thought about modifying some of the compost pit ideas I have read about by building a concrete or concrete block compost pit in the side of a fairly steep bank or hill. I know that compost containers that are sunk into the ground should have no bottoms, of course, and that they should have crushed stone or gravel near their base. Otherwise water will have nowhere to drain. After a heavy rain the compost would get soggy and smelly and there would be very little to prevent it from staying that way.

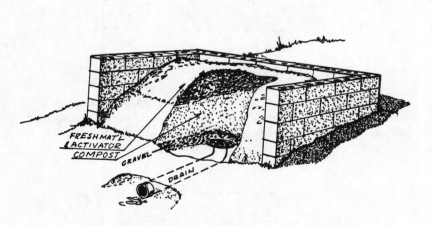

What would happen if you installed a drain in the bottom of a sunken compost container and ran a pipe to a lower basin further down the hill which would collect the compost water? This fertile juice, compost tea, would be a treat for vegetable plants if it was used as a side dressing and would provide wonderful nourishment for tiny plants in seed flats. It seems to me that this would be a near perfect system. Almost nothing would be lost through leaching. What do you think?

BARRELS, DRUMS, AND GARBAGE CANS

Old fifty-five gallon oil drums, barrels and garbage cans make excellent containers for small composting systems. You can make compost water in an oil drum, for instance, by filling one quarter of the drum with old manure and filling the rest with water. Stir this brew every once in a while if you are strolling past the drum and happen to think of it. After a couple of months dip a bucket or watering can into the drum when you want strong compost tea.

A friend of mine in Stowe, Vermont has developed a slightly more sophisticated way of making the same stuff — without stirring. He also uses a doctored-up fifty-five gallon oil drum which is set on

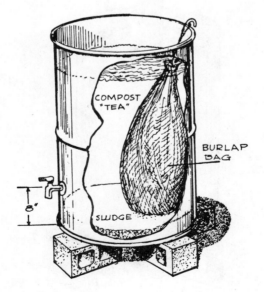

cinder blocks. He puts some compost into a burlap bag, ties off the top of the bag with twine, puts the bag in the drum which is already filled with water, and fastens the twine to a hook that is welded to the outside of the drum near the top.

About eight inches from the *bottom* of the drum there is an old faucet which has also been welded into the side of the steel container. Through this he can draw off compost water as he needs it. My friend points out that it is important that the faucet not be placed any lower than six or eight inches from the bottom of the barrel. "Sludge" from the big burlap tea bag will settle to the bottom of the barrel making a bed of residue four to six inches deep. This can clog the faucet. These dregs need to be cleaned out every three years or so, and they make wonderful fertilizer. He uses it on the garden while his wife applies the compost tea to houseplants and seedlings with a kitchen baster.

For composting on a *very* small scale — and in a very small space such as a corner of your garage — try this method: It is pretty easy to cut holes in the bottom of a steel drum. A high speed drill or a cold

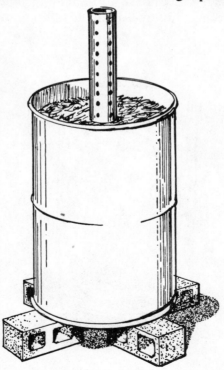

chisel work best. If you don't have or can't borrow either of these, use an old hatchet or axe. But don't chop! Hold one corner of the axe's cutting edge against the metal bottom of the drum and hit it sharply with a hammer. The metal should puncture easily. After a second hammer blow you should have a nice elongated hole. And I think you will be surprised at how little damage you will have done to the axe blade.

When you feel you have made enough ventilation-drainage holes, set the drum on blocks of some kind to let air come in underneath it. Then build thin layers of leaves, garbage, grass and activator into the can, stick a three or four-foot section of perforated pipe into the center of the pile for ventilation, and leave it standing vertically. Wet down the whole works and let it sit for six weeks or so, before you turn it.

You can do the same sort of thing by drilling holes in wooden barrels or kegs (though these may be too valuable as antique items these days) and in metal or even plastic garbage pails. A coping saw, keyhole saw or portable jigsaw can help you cut out the base of a plastic container in just a few minutes. Lay a piece of chicken wire or hardware cloth — almost any gauge will do — on some bricks or two-by-fours for support and set the bottomless can on top of the screen, so air can come in and water can go out. It might not be a bad idea to drill some air holes in the top of the can too — if it has one.

Put about four inches of coarse dry material in the bottom of the can, then add a layer of garbage, some alfalfa meal or some other natural high-nitrogen activator, then some leaves, some wood ashes, some more garbage and perhaps a little soil. The organic matter should retain just the right amount of moisture. Excess water, which might make the fixings in the can become anaerobic, will run out the bottom. It will of course wash away some "goodies" as it goes, so try not to water any more than is necessary.

EARTHWORM BOXES

I have often wondered how I could make better use of garbage in the wintertime. It has been suggested to me on a number of occasions that I build an earthworm box in my cellar. This has struck me as an appealing idea because I have always thought it a colossal bore to have to put on my boots again after supper and tramp through three feet of snow to empty the garbage outside. I haven't built one yet, but I am going to someday.

It would be a simple thing, I figure, to construct a seven-foot by three-foot box with six-inch sides from one single four-by-eight sheet of three-quarter inch marine plywood. This could be set on saw horses, lined with polyethylene perhaps, and filled with fairly dry soil — not mud.

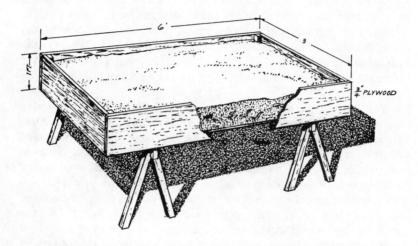

Earthworms could be "planted" in the box, and they could be fed fresh garbage each day. It could be chopped in the blender using a minimal amount of water to prevent excess wetness. An earthworm box should stay moist and dank — certainly no problem in *my* cellar — but it should never get soggy.

I am a great admirer of these "intestines of the soil", but I have to keep reminding myself that earthworms do have certain limitations. They have no teeth, for instance. There is no way they can bit off more than they can chew. They have difficulty ingesting anything that is much larger than the size of their mouths. Chopping gives them a break in this respect. While I was feeding them garbage I might throw in a tasty pinch of manure — the dried packaged kind probably, for obvious reasons — and a dash of some partially digested compost from the dormant wintertime heap. I think that I would also provide a cover to keep light out of the box if it were to be put in some bright place. Earthworms do not seem to relish illumination.

Leave them to their own devices and earthworms will manufacture compost in about sixty days, depending of course on the size of their population. They will produce castings that look very much like coffee grounds. These should be richer by about five times than the most fertile soil, and loaded with microorganisms. I have heard it said that they are twice as rich in calcium as good loam, seven times richer in phosphorous and eleven times richer in potassium. The *Reader's Digest* tells me that actinomycetes multiplies seven times as it passes through the body of an earthworm. Earthworm castings are black gold. I am really missing the boat by not hosting some of them in my home. I will next winter for sure!

To save these worthy creatures for further duties in another box, spread the finished compost on a tarp and allow it to sit in the sun. The worms, sensing heat, light and dryness, will cluster together in sticky balls, just the way they will in a bait box or worm can that you have allowed to get too dry. It is easy to pick them up and put them somewhere else where they can get on with their work.

PLASTIC BAGS

People are doing winter composting in the most unlikely places these days — in cellars, garages, even in attics and closets. Garbage and nearly any other kind of organic matter can be decomposed in those green thirty-two gallon trash can liners. The process *is* anaerobic, but there need be no odor if the bag is kept tightly sealed. Best of all, there is absolutely no danger of leaching with this method.

Put one or two shovelsful of debris into the bag and sprinkle in some simple activator. Then repeat until the bag is about four-fifths full. Dribble in about two quarts of water, shake and gently knead the bag to mix the liquid with the other materials as best you can. Seal off the bags and hang them somewhere out of the way or throw them in a back corner and forget about them. There should be no need for further mixing or turning of any kind.

Almost nothing in the way of microbial digestion will happen if the material in the bag gets too cold or freezes. This is why trashbag composting will not work outside, in an unheated barn, woodshed or other outbuilding. When you need compost it is time to open the bags. But be sure you take them out of the house first. Stand back, hold your nose, and dump the contents on the ground. Spread and fluff the material so that it gets exposed to lots of oxygen. The stench should soon disappear.

THE CLIVUS TOILET

The Clivus (pronounced Klē-vus) toilet is a device designed to safely compost human excrement and other wastes right in the home. It has been developed by a Swedish company, Clivus Multrum, Inc.

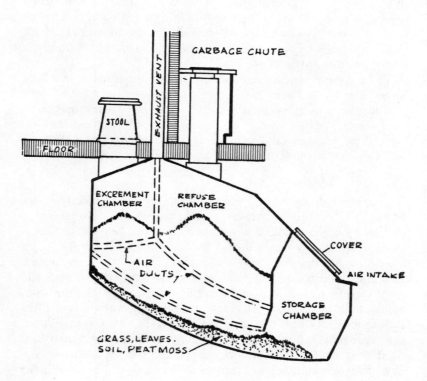

This exciting system has a number of advantages:

(1) It conserves fresh water, a necessity that we are running out of more rapidly than a lot of us would like to believe. A conventional toilet uses — and wastes — horrendous amounts of water. Do you know you use about seven gallons of water each time you flush?

(2) It causes no pollution. A home with a Clivus toilet needs no septic tank, leach field or connections with a city sewage system. There is no danger of run-off into fresh water supplies.

(3) It permits valuable human wastes to be returned to the soil. In this sense the Clivus is an important breakthrough. It offers a heretofore unfound way to virtually eliminate pathogenic organisms in composted "night soil", and allows its use even where vegetables are to be grown.

(4) It reduces energy consumption. In many homes the water pump is a major energy hog, and it spends a large portion of its working time pumping water to keep conventional toilet tanks filled.

The Clivus has three basic elements: a garbage chute installed in a kitchen cabinet or counter top, a toilet stool, and a big sloping fiberglass digester that is installed in the basement of the home. The decomposition that takes place in the digester is very slow and very thorough — taking months, even years. There is no odor because of the carefully designed ventilation system, and compost from the digester can be emptied as infrequently as once a year under normal use by a family of four. The Clivus literature emphasizes that the humus taken out of the digester is a very rich and safe garden compost. Whether or not it is *completely* safe remains to be seen. There is always the chance that some unknown and unhealthy viruses may survive. It would probably be best to keep it away from root crops until further research is done. For more detailed information about the Clivus toilet write to the Rockefeller Family Association, Room 5500, 30 Rockefeller Plaza, New York, N.Y. 10020 or the Garden Way Living Center, 1186 Williston Road, So. Burlington, Vermont 05401.

SHEET COMPOSTING AND
GREEN MANURING

Sheet composting and green manuring are the primary alternative methods for getting vast amounts of organic matter into your garden's soil. They are certainly more direct because, in a sense, you are eliminating the middle man, the compost pile itself. No nutrients can be lost through leaching as they inevitably must be to a certain extent from a compost heap. At the same time, there is no possibility of thermal kill and no way that weed seeds can be killed *en masse* without using strong chemicals.

Sheet composting is sometimes confused with mulching. When you mulch you feed the soil slowly if you are using organic matter, but your main interest is in protecting the soil from weeds, too much heat or too much evaporation by laying something on the *surface* of the ground. Sheet composting involves *mixing* organic material with the soil itself, usually with the help of a spade or some sort of machine like a disc harrow or rototiller. A rotary tiller with tines in the rear does this best for the average home gardener. It chops the material as it integrates it with the soil particles.

To use a rototiller as a sheet composting machine you simply spread leaves, manure — or whatever other organic matter you can gather, buy or scavenge — on your garden, set the machine to maximum tilling depth, and till everything under. This is an ideal way to quickly improve soils that contain too much clay, sand, gravel or builder's fill. It will also help to protect garden spots that are threatened by erosion.

Leaves, as you know, abound in trace elements. Green grass clippings contain all kinds of nitrogen and need not be dried before being tilled under. Almost any kind of healthy organic matter, in fact, will provide nourishment for the earthworms and micro-organisms in the garden.

Your soil will gratefully accept and even acknowledge all the sheet compost you can give it by producing more nutritious vegetables. Last fall a neighbor and trusted friend borrowed my pick-up truck and my two children for an afternoon.

My friend has a tiny garden plot (it can't be more than twelve feet by forty), but his careful management allows him to grow a surprising abundance of vegetables. He lives on ledge and had to bring in topsoil in order to have a graden at all.

Together with my two, and two children of his own, he drove slowly around the nearby countryside loading all the leaves he could find and easily rake up into the back of the truck. Each time he made a stop he asked the kids to jump and play in the leaves. Naturally they were delighted to oblige. When the leaves got pretty well packed down, he told them to sit down while he drove to find more. He harvested three truckloads this way, which with the fine method of compaction he used must have amounted to a dozen or more loads.

Later that quiet Sunday afternoon I finally began to wonder what had become of the children. I wandered down the road until I could **hear screams of delight coming from behind** my **neighbor's house.**

When I got closer I could see the four young ones still romping and wrestling in the leaves, which by this time lay a foot and a half or two feet thick on top of the garden.

My friend was just coming around the corner of the barn with the rear-end tiller. I really doubted that he would be able to till *all* those leaves into the garden. But sure enough, after three or four passes with the machine, most of them were buried — much to the disgust of four very dirty youngsters. This spring every remnant of the leaves has disappeared, and my friend's little garden seems to have at least two or three inches more soil than it had last year.

Green manures are *not* those that have come fresh from the cow or horse — as so many people have tried to tell me. They are cover crops like buckwheat or rye. Green manuring is sheet composting with living green matter that grows right in place. Turning under crop residues such as corn stalks, tomato vines, pea plants or thick rooted crops like kale is also green manuring.

Growing cover crops for the express purpose of turning them under is best done either in the off-growing season (ryegrass will show good growth in the fall and early spring) or in some portion of the garden that is left fallow. Roots of green manure crops will grow deep into the subsoil retrieving nutrients that have leached beyond the reach of many vegetable plants' roots.

Legumes like peas, beans, soybeans, cow peas, alfalfa, clover and vetch are easy to plant and are especially valuable because they attract nitrogen-fixing bacteria to their roots and in this way contribute nitrogen to the soil. Other green manures like buckwheat, annual and perennial ryegrass, oats, wheat, sorghum and — yes — common weeds, all will literally add tons of good organic material to your garden. Try it. A helpful Garden Way Publishing bulletin by cover-crop expert Dick Raymond is called A-5 *Cover Crop Gardening.*

9

The End Product

A LL right, the inevitable question, "How do we know when compost is done, and how long does it take?" I will have to admit, right off the bat, that the second part of this question is probably more difficult to answer. In a way, asking how long it takes to make compost is like wanting to know the exact date of the last killing frost in the spring. Clearly these are two of life's little unpredictables.

Because there are so many "ifs" involved, there can only be some general guidelines as far as any sort of a composting timetable is concerned. We have already seen that *if* you are just starting out, and *if* you have the right equipment — such as a shredder — fourteen-day compost can be made à la the University of California method. *If,* on the other hand, you have more time, it may be better to wait longer for your compost. Perhaps you and yours generate enough waste around your home to have several compost piles going at once, and can afford to let fermentation go on for two years or more the way Samuel Ogden does.

Four to six months seems to be the normal amount of time needed to make superior compost here in the northeastern United States. *If* we were to start a pile in November, it would take somewhat longer than that. *If* we were to start one in June, *if* we attended to it faithfully, and *if* we turned it carefully and regularly, it might take less time than that. *If* you live in a climate that is warmer than ours, closer to that of Indore, you can probably do a satisfactory job of composting most kinds of organic matter in the three months that Sir Albert Howard recommends. The safest bet is to think in terms of giving the compost a chance to decompose for a *longer* time than seems necessary.

Here, as I see them, are several characteristics of ideal "finished" compost:

- It should be free of nearly all pathogenic organisms and weed seeds.

- It should have an adequate supply of at least some of the major nutrients, and should contain a variety of minor nutrients. Hopefully the final product will show traces of manganese, boron, sodium, zinc and other elements. If you had enough compost to spread over your entire garden each year you should, in a fairly short time, be able to correct magnesium, copper, iron, and boron deficiencies in the soil. This does not mean — you will remember — that in all cases compost is a complete fertilizer which needs no further chemical supplements.

- Finished compost should be "crumbly." "Crumbly" is another one of those vague terms like "well-rotted manure," "friable soil" and "tilth," which gardeners so often use. It was a long time before I was able to learn what this meant. "Ripened" compost does not need to be decomposed to the point of being colloidal — almost powdery like Sam Ogden's. It should be sort of fluffy — not stringy. Tough, highly-carbonaceous things like straw fibers, for example, may still be intact. But if the compost is ready for use, you should be able to crush and pulverize material like this between your finger tips. Crumbly compost, like crumbly soil, allows air to penetrate, holds moisture well, but allows excess water to drain away.

- Finished compost is dark in color. Like earthworm castings, good compost has been called "black gold." If it is *truly* black — rather than deep brown — and has a greasy texture, it may also be called "black butter." Black butter is usually the product of a too-moist anaerobic compost system, and is less desirable than the aerobically-produced stuff.

• Though it may not look exactly like earth, good finished compost should *smell* sweet and earthy — never moldy and rotten.

• It will have undergone a drop in temperature from somewhere near 150 degree Fahrenheit, to whatever the temperature is outside the compost pile. Compost that is still much warmer than the surrounding air needs more decomposition time.

• The best standard for judging a compost's state of completion — which cannot be done without special analysis equipment — is by measuring the C/N. It should be somewhere in the vicinity of 14-20, approaching that of pure humus (10).

• It should still consist of at least twenty-five to fifty percent organic matter. In this sense it is even more valuable than actual manure. Not only is the percentage of organic matter higher, but it holds far less moisture than fresh manure.

COMPOST AND SOIL IMPROVEMENT

According to H. H. Koepf, "Good compost can be applied in any amount at any time on any crop." He will get little argument from me on that score, although I would perhaps elaborate on his remark a *little*. Compost will do much to improve your soil's structure. The organic matter it contains will of course improve the earth's ability to hold water and retain oxygen.

Fortunately, compost is by definition a composite of different ingredients, some of which will rot more rapidly than others. This is good. Actually, if everything were to decompose at the same speed, the end product would not be so valuable. Because certain types of matter, such as lignin and cellulose, break down more slowly than others, nutrients will continue to be released over a longer period of time. The soil into which it is put should *maintain* its crumbly characteristic for as long as it takes for the hard-to-rot things to disappear altogether. Crumbly soil is, of course, best for plants, because it is riddled with air spaces where tiny roots can grow without any difficulty.

Compost continues contributing to the garden soil even after all of the organic matter it contained *has* rotted away. You already know that by adding compost you are literally injecting life into your garden by adding a multitude of helpful microorganisms. Some of these will be "fixing" bacteria which will emplant nitrogen on the soil, while others will be manufacturing antibiotics to protect your plants from various diseases.

Compost that is almost completely decomposed comes close to what Dr. Ehrenfried Pfeiffer calls "stable humus." "Stability" implies that the substance can no longer break down rapidly, since the degradable organic matter as such has all but disappeared. From this point on, further decomposition must be very gradual. Now the large population of microbes will start to die. Lots of valuable organic compounds are "locked up" in their microscopic bodies. Once the proper conditions of moisture, oxygen and temperature are just right, *they* will start to decompose, and these organic compounds can be released into the soil.

The most advantageous time to incorporate large volumes of compost into the garden is in the fall. Spread whatever compost you have been making over the summer over the entire growing area. You can do this any time after the first killing frost and before the soil becomes frozen hard. It is not a requirement that it be turned or tilled right into the garden. It will do the soil a lot of good if you just let it lie there over the winter. If you do have the right equipment, a rototiller or a small garden tractor with a harrow, or if you are an ambitious soul when it comes to spading by hand, you will be doing your garden even more good if you mix the compost in with the soil particles. Compost that simply sits on top of the garden may dry out too quickly, and some of the nutrients it contains may escape into the atmosphere as gases.

This brings to mind the problem of compost storage. It is hard to "put compost by" effectively. A pile of rich, rotted organic matter will keep for a *while* if it is covered with plastic or a canvas tarp to discourage leaching. As a general rule, however, it is a better practice to put compost into the garden too early, perhaps before it is fully "completed," rather than too late. If allowed to sit around for too long after it is "finished" it may lose much of its value. The further the materials are allowed to decompose — without the addition of some fresh, fibrous organic matter — the more colloidal the compost becomes as it breaks down into smaller and smaller-sized pieces. This in itself is not necessarily bad. The problem is that it is difficult for air to penetrate any great distance through such a fine aggregate, and anaerobia may be the result. Don't leave a pile of finished compost unused for more than half a year or so at the most.

If you happen to have a batch of compost that is ripening in the spring, and it appears that you are not going to be adding further material as the summer progresses, there is no need to wait until fall before you use it. Finished or nearly-finished compost is fairly effective if it is used about a month before planting time in the spring. It can be broadcast and worked into the soil at that time. Besides offering fertilizer to the garden and conditioning the soil, the compost will have even more value because it retains heat from the sun much better than most ordinary garden soil.

Some say that composting in the springtime will rob nitrogen from soil as the compost continues to decompose. This same source also recommended against using compost as a mulch around growing plants, for the same reason. I have never found this to be the case with compost, although I have never taken any accurate measurements of the C/N in soil before and after compost was added to it. Even so, it seems safe to assume that the C/N of even partially-rotted, "unstable" compost should be low enough so that no nitrogen should have to be borrowed from the surrounding earth. Nitrogen supplement *would* be necessary, however, if you tilled in a lot of *un-*composted hay or straw, which would have a high carbon content. I would say add finished compost to your soil or use compost as a mulch anytime — especially in the hottest, driest periods of mid-summer. You should never have to worry about nitrogen deficiency in garden plants if you do.

The question is sometimes raised: Is it possible to get *too* much organic matter into the soil? The answer is yes, it probably *is* possible, particularly if all of the organic matter you were to use was all of one kind and was highly carbonaceous. You could throw the carbon-nitrogen ratio so far out of balance that the soil might have a hard time growing much of anything. If you *saturated* a given piece of land with some sort of highly acidic organic material, you might seriously influence that soil's pH for a while. In ninety-nine percent of the cases, though, where compost is the organic matter in question, worrying too much about excessive organic material in the soil is like warning a starving man about the dangers of obesity.

COMPOST FOR PLANTING

Don't spread and turn under your entire supply of compost all at once. Save a little to use with some of your plantings. Because compost does not contain *everything* plants need for their nutrition, it is not a good idea to plant most vegetables in pure compost alone. I doubt very much, as a matter of fact, that the pole bean sprout which got started in my compost pile could have continued its frightening rate of growth.

I am told that right after germination is the time when very young plants are most likely to suffer from undernourishment. The seedling has not had time to send out a very extensive root system at that point. Pure loam, or even a combination of loam and compost, is likely to lack some nutrients — particularly phosphorous. It is not a bad idea to add a *little* fertilizer to compost at this time.

But be careful. Try to plan far enough ahead so that this can be done well in advance of whenever your seeds are to be planted. This will give the particles of fertilizer time to dissolve in the damp compost, and give the chemicals time to work their way in among the particles of organic matter. Be sure that you use no more than *half* of the fertilizer you might normally use to sidedress a particular plant or spread over a certain area of garden space.

I have found that compost which has no fertilizer added will never burn seeds, even if seeds are sown directly on top of it. The same is true of "inoculated" compost, if the fertilizer has been added well beforehand. I am sure that pure organic gardening and natural-foods fans would regard the practice of mixing together compost and commercial fertilizers as the worst kind of horticultural heresy. But soil scientist Emil Truog has made some interesting remarks along these lines in an article called "Organic Compost or Commercial Fertilizer — Which?" that appeared in *Handbook on Soils*. He writes,

> Some advocates of "organic only" hold that fertility elements in commercial fertilizers having been made through the use of strong acids like sulfuric and nitric acids, or consisting of inorganic salts like potassium chloride, are corrosive or toxic to bacteria and earthworms, and even give rise to crops of inferior food value, causing disease in animals and humans. There exists absolutely no scientific evidence to support this contention. Experiments have shown that the application of commercial fertilizers tends to increase the numbers of bacteria and earthworms in soils.
>
> When organic matter rots in the soil through the action of bacteria, nitrogen is changed largely to nitric acid, sulfur largely to sulfuric acid and so on. These acids then combine with elements (like calcium) in the soil to form salts, which serve as nutrients for plants . . .
>
> There is absolutely no difference between the nitric and sulfuric acids formed in the soil from organic matter through the action of bacteria and those same acids as used in a fertilizer factory. The same holds for many other chemicals, for example calcium nitrate or potassium chloride. Thus we see that the form in which plants take up their nutrients is much the same whether they are originally supplied as organic material such as compost, or as commercial fertilizer.

Compost with a bit of fertilizer added is great for use as a potting compound in starter flats. The most common practice among people who use compost in their greenhouses seems to be to make a mixture of one-third compost, one-third soil, and one-third coarse sand, perlite or vermiculite. Ideally, the compost should first be sifted through a screen or shredded very fine. We keep a small electric shredder in our greenhouse for just this purpose.

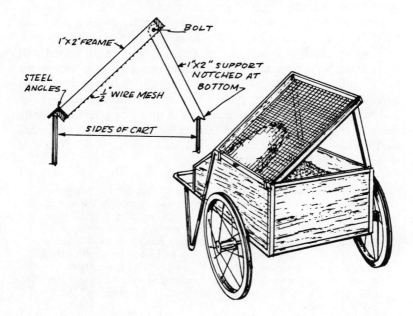

The sand or vermiculite in the potting mixture should help the compound in the pot or seed flat to drain. We even put gravel or crushed stone in the bottom of the larger pots or empty milk cartons where we transplant larger tomato seedlings.

Later, as we get ready to transplant tomatoes in the garden proper, we dig a furrow anywhere from four to six inches deep and fill it about half full of rich garbage compost. We water-soak the compost-soil-sand mixture in the milk carton or seed flat, and remove the young plant — trying to keep the soil surrounding its roots as much intact as possible. We remove all but the uppermost leaves on the plant, and lay the roots and long stem down in the furrow on top of the compost. We cover them with soil, leaving only the few remaining leaves sticking out of the ground. The stem, fed by the rich compost, will start to grow tiny root hairs almost immediately, and within a couple of weeks the stem will have transformed itself into a long and complicated tangle of roots.

This makes a very strong foundation from which the rest of the plant can grow healthy and well nourished. Peppers are usually planted in the same row, interspaced with the tomatoes as companion plants. They are set outstanding upright on the compost, not lying down.

When I plant pole beans in my own garden, I follow a procedure which is much like the method described by Sam Ogden in *Step-by Step to Organic Vegetable Growing*. I dig a row of holes about three feet apart, eight inches deep and two feet in diameter. Then, with a crowbar, I poke a much deeper and smaller hole, and set the bean pole — a straight stick seven or eight feet long cut from the woods near home — in the center of the larger hole.

I fill the bigger hole with a compost-and-fertilizer mixture and lay a circle of seeds right on top of the compost. Each seed is about eight inches away from the pole. A ninth seed is set in the middle of the circle, right next to the pole — mostly for good luck. About an inch of loose soil is put over the top of the seeds and tamped down by hand. Early plantings of "Romano" or "Kentucky Wonder" beans seem to germinate more quickly in compost than those planted in regular soil. The roots of the young plants have no difficulty finding their way down into the loose organic matter and are able to draw goodness from it right away. Soon the leaves are very large and dark green, and, in time, the beans superb.

We sometimes use the same technique when we plant hills of corn, cucumbers or squash — leaving out the pole, naturally. Peas, beans of all kinds, grapes, lettuce, cabbage, cauliflower, broccoli, raspberries, Brussels sprouts, chard, spinach and other greens can be planted with compost too. It hardly takes any longer than planting or transplanting the conventional way. It is simply a matter of making a shallow trench or hole with a hoe, shovel or furrower, putting compost in the depression, laying the seeds on the compost, covering them and firming the soil.

Perennials like asparagus and rhubarb will do well if their roots are planted on top of a much deeper trench — say eight inches wide and a foot and a half deep — which has been filled with fertilized compost. To plant strawberries we sometimes build a little mound of compost in the bottom of a shallow furrow, and drape the roots of the young plant over the mound so they cover it like a skirt. Then we bring the soil up to the plant just below the crown. Root crops like carrots, beets, turnips, rutabagas and the rest might "dampen-off" — become susceptible to certain fungus-inspired diseases if they are planted too early in too much compost. The best way to help them is to thoroughly integrate compost with the soil in the space where they will be grown. Rototillage will do this job nicely.

Last year a group of our neighbors who own a tennis court collectively decided that they should turn their clay court — too wet to play on too much of the time — into a hard-surface, all-weather court. The contractor dug up the old clay and asked permission to deposit it in a clearing among some trees not far from us. We agreed. He spread it around carefully, so as not to harm the roots of any of the trees, and smoothed it with a bulldozer. By the time he had finished, the little clearing seemed such an attractive garden spot, that we and one of our other neighbors decided to see if we could eventually grow something there to reinforce what our small gardens at home produced.

This decision was made with only moderate enthusiasm because we knew that the soil the contractor had put there was the stickiest kind of clay — totally devoid, as far as we could see, of any sort of organic matter. To make matters worse, a simple pH test revealed that it was quite alkaline, possibly the result of some lime-based "hardener" they may have been put on the court or of some other chemicals designed to keep down the dust during dry summer days. All signs seemed to indicate that this place in the woods was going to be a desert — for a few years at least — unless we took some sort of drastic steps to improve the soil. Initial long-range plans called for a multi-year program of green manuring — buckwheat in summer, ryegrass in the fall — to build up the earthworm, microbe and organic matter content.

After a few days of dry late-May weather the old tennis court material changed from gluey mud which accumulated on my shoe soles after three steps, to concrete-like hardpan where I could leave *no* tracks. I spent one whole evening turning it up with our powerful rear-end tiller, thinking that I was getting it ready for a planting of buckwheat. The tiller and I did such a nice job of loosening the tough clay that the old court again began to take on the look of a potential garden. It looked so much that way in the unclear dusk that my wife asked optimistically, "Say, what would happen if we planted some vegetables here this year?"

Why not? In the cold light of dawn, things looked less promising, but we forged ahead making furrows with the help of the tiller again. We filled the furrows with some second-rate compost we had made at home from leaves and spoiled hay. By midmorning the noise of our labor had attracted a crowd of neighbors and we put everyone to work. Suddenly we had a community garden. Together we planted corn, lettuce, several kinds of chard, beets, soybeans, Chinese cabbage, cucumbers, peas, bush beans, radishes, winter and summer squash. The seeds were laid on top of the rotted organic matter, the rows covered with loose soil and carefully walked upon by many children's sneakers. Then a small amount of 16-10-20 fertilizer was sprinkled over the top of each row. It turned out to be a rather festive Saturday morning. Even so, no one really held high hopes for the success of the garden.

Less than a week later, after a rain shower or two, radishes which had been planted along with other seeds to mark the rows, were up and going strong. And a week after that nearly everything else we planted had put in an appearance too. To our surprise and delight, the seed germination must have been close to 100 percent. It was so complete that plantings made too close together by some of the kids had to be thinned.

By now we are growing such a fine crop of vegetables that some of the people in the neighborhood dread the possibility of being slaves to freezer bags, pressure cookers and canning jars during the months of August and September. Our little desert clearing is bearing fruit, and with tongue in cheek everyone is suddenly blaming me for all of the work I have provided.

Now each of us is going to have to cultivate and weed another garden besides our own, and we may fight about who harvests what. We are going to have to collect leaves in the fall, sheet compost them, and plant winter rye. If local bands of raccoons and squirrels are able to do what the woodchucks and rabbits have failed to do so far — discover our secret plot in the woods —they may feast on our ripened corn. If they do, and I fear they will, we will probably have to build a fence for next year.

Such are the dubious rewards of success, however ill-planned. A headache, sometimes, this self-sufficient living. A lot of work too. Satisfying though. Satisfying, indeed. And I can't help but wonder if this minor first-year triumph with an old tennis court would really have been possible without the compost . . .

10

Further Ramblings

FUTURISM, trying to forecast upcoming events and speculating about man's prospects here on earth, has become very fashionable lately. It has grown out of the gypsy soothsayer's tent, away from the astrological horoscope that appears in the daily newspaper, out of the mystery-shrouded seance and into the more academic environs of the university and the intellectual journal.

Ecologists, economists, medical people, historians, psychologists and sociologists now program "trends", as they see them, into a computer and ask the machine to project the snowballing effects of human consumption rates and other related activities like pollution and population growth, into the years to come. Measuring these projections against known supplies of resources, researchers are usually led to startling and cataclysmic conclusions such as those found in the famous *Limits to Growth,* a frightening treatise put out by "The Club of Rome", a group of intellectuals at M.I.T.

The most disheartening part of this whole game is that so many of these predictions hold so little hope for us. What nearly all the computer print-outs seem to be saying — some more forcefully than others — is that we have made some serious if not irrevocable mistakes with our environment, that we have continually misjudged mother earth as an endless cornucopia of raw materials, that we are, in short, in big trouble.

Some experts even suggest that social, political and economic consequences of such dire proportions will be upon us so quickly that we may have no chance of coping with them. The sudden and astronomical increase in fertilizer prices alone creates its own special kind of "future shock," which *forces* us to realize how fast the world is running out of phosphorous and other vital minerals.

If you are exposed to enough of this kind of pessimistic thinking — John Maddox, editor of the British journal, *Nature,* has labeled it "The Doomsday Syndrome" — your inclination is to start hanging out black crepe and begin mourning for the human race. But we might console ourselves by rationalizing that things may not be *that* bad yet. Maddox is certainly correct when he warns us about the dangers of over dramatizing our common destiny and tries to persuade us to resist the urge to cry "Wolf! Wolf!" too loud and too often.

If in the first place the proverbial wolf *is,* in fact, about to devour our flock, we may find that our cries for help receive no satisfactory answers, simply because there is no one out there who can be of much help. We have to look to ourselves. Our own good conscience and common sense may turn out to be the biggest and most valuable natural resource of all when things get really tough. In the second place, we should not waver in our faith that it is *not* too late to discover and implement some solutions to the problems of overpopulation, famine, depletion of the world's mineral resources and the rest.

If things get bad enough soon enough, shortages and inequities may force things to the point where human survival depends on selecting — either by war or through simple neglect — who is going to live and who is going to be permitted to die. Of course we all hope that this never comes to pass, but it *is* a distinct possibility we should all be facing one way or another. Thoughtful and responsible people seem to recognize this "clear and present danger," and in many cases are preparing to meet it head on, on a direct personal level.

Others who are beginning to think like them, play their own futuristic games. They foresee only some of us making it through the "crunch" — their euphemism for the time when all economic, social and political hell breaks loose. Those who *do* make it through, they say, will be those who have become less dependent on our complex economic system as it now exists, those who have "returned to a simpler life," those who have learned to fend for themselves by acquiring certain survival skills like basic carpentry, vegetable gardening, animal husbandry, elementary mechanics, masonry, inventive recycling and compost making, which dramatically reduces the need for purchased fertilizer.

Many individual "homesteads" which represent sincere efforts on the part of folks to deal with the question of how to live reasonably comfortably and reasonably happily in a future which looks uncertain at best.

Not all of us may necessarily want to adopt the homestead lifestyle which some choose, but we can learn a great deal from some of these people about coping with the future. They have already played a large role in the grass roots movement that has inspired a more thorough exploration of alternative energy sources, the interest in growing and preserving food on the home place, the revival of some nearly lost arts, crafts and living techniques, and the development of toned-down technology which can address itself to the small-scale problems which soon we may all have to face each day.

Now we are hearing more than the "wind in the willows," the traditional songs of the birds, and the slapping of waves against our shores. We are seeing beyond the "purple mountains' majesty" and more than the obvious sunshine on a picture-postcard field of flowers.

We are awakening to some of the important things which are closer to where we live. More of us are beginning to sense vibrations from the nonvisible creatures in our soil. We can almost hear the inaudible growing sounds made by our green plants on a summer afternoon. We can almost feel the imperceptible, continuous and helpful munching and crunching of insects in our compost and in the forest floor. We are learning to admire simple earthy things like the granular leavings of a friendly earthworm. We are learning to hail the passing armies of bacteria which we are beginning to see as frequent allies more than as just dirty germs. We are getting to know fungi as healthy things and are realizing that rotting is as consistent with growing as sowing is with harvesting.

We are becoming more and more aware of ourselves too, more conscious of each other, I think, and of the entire natural and cultural milieu in which we live. We are starting to understand that the problems we face as individuals extend to all corners of the earth. No place and no one is exempt. As a gentle friend said to me recently, "Economically, things are getting pretty bad, yet people are acting as though they are high on living. I see more kindness and love and real communication. People seem to be trying to compete with each other less and are getting involved with each other more." If he is right —simplistic as it may sound — our growing love and empathy for each other may be one of the things that saves us.

Another more practical — and not incompatible — salvation may be to turn some of the mistakes we have made to our advantage; to use some of the large-scale aspects of our socio-political structure and technology to help us move past the point of *talking* about efficient recycling to actually *reclaiming* some of the resources we are wasting and thereby losing. We are already the largest mass producers of waste in the world, about 1600 pounds per family of four per year, to say nothing of municipal and industrial wastes —and we don't know what to do with it all.

If we can no longer continue to mass-produce fertilizer at the present rate, why aren't we giving more thought to mass producing compost? "Composting," according to municipal composting expert Stanley Bulpitt, "is not the same as disposal. It turns a glut into a product." Despite the fact that a composting plant in Auckland, New Zealand has proven that it can be done profitably, many persist in their arguments that a composting facility cannot consistently operate in the black.

"We've thought about it," they say. "It is not cost effective — not economically feasible. There is no profit in it." This is "pure economics" — the old school of thinking which insists on continual "progress," reckless and irresponsible consumption of raw materials high profit margins and growth factors. It is the kind of economics which no longer applies. It is the kind of inhuman and selfish economics which got us into trouble in the first place, and in spite of what so many unenlightened people may still be saying, this kind of squandering attitude will not and cannot get us back *out* of trouble, because it denies the obvious importance of reusing and conserving what we already have.

This is not to suggest that anyone should be running a community-sized composting operation or recycling plant at a loss, as an energy sink, or as some sort of poorly planned grand ecological experiment. There are going to be problems — sanitary ones, technical ones, and financial ones. And this illustrates the need, as some have already suggested, for a strong national or even international composting association which could coordinate research, eliminate duplication of effort, and direct us toward the establishment of a serious composting industry — sometime before the world's supply of phosphorous disappears altogether.

Such an industry would be producing a valuable, marketable product, not necessarily one that is sold as a "complete" fertilizer, but one that is sold on its merits as nature's most perfect soil conditioner and stimulant to soil life.

If it is not magnifying the importance of composting too much to say it, making compost — either individually or collectively — enriches our lives almost as much as it does our gardens, because doing it seems to harmonize our being here with the way the world ought to be. To say it all in one quick breath: composting can make you feel good about yourself. If you don't already know it, you'll see.

Other Garden Way Publishing Books You Will Enjoy

Zucchini Cookbook. At last — Nancy Ralston & Marynor Jordan describe wonderful things to do with zucchini! Everything from zucchini marmalade to zucchini raisin pie with over 250 recipes. $5.95. Order #107-8.

Carrots Love Tomatoes. Our strange but true, companion planting book by Louise Riotte tells what to plant together for outstanding results and why. $7.95. Order #064-0.

Down-to-Earth Vegetable Gardening Know-How. Peppers, Matchsticks + Epsom Salts! Vermont's Master Gardener, Dick Raymond grows peppers the size of cantaloupes with a simple matchstick and epsom salt trick. $7.95. Order #271-6.

Wood Heat Safety. Jay Shelton, recognized expert on wood combustion. "In this detailed, very specific book, he considers virtually every detail. A commendably good job in every way; you needn't wait for a better one to come along." *The New Whole Earth Catalog*. $9.95. Order #160-4.

The Garden Way Bread Book. Fabulous collection of 140 original recipes by Ellen Johnson. "Can't fail" instructions for a tasty loaf! Over 100 illus. and photos. 102 pp., $9.95. Order #139-6.

The Pleasure of Herbs. Phyllis Shaudys's month-by-month guide to growing, using, and enjoying herbs. Full of crafts, lore, recipes, and growing information. A favorite of herb lovers across North America. $13.95. Order #423-9.

Compact House Book. These winning designs edited by Don Metz prove that houses with 1,000 or fewer sq. ft. of floor space can be imaginative, comfortable, inviting places to live. Each design includes rendering, floor plans, site plan, estimated building cost, etc. $14.95. Order #323-2.

Raising Rabbits the Modern Way. Revised Edition. Our best seller by Bob Bennett for home and semicommercial breeders includes breed selection, housing, feeding, disease prevention, marketing and much more. $8.95. Order #479-4.

Broccoli & Company. Over 100 healthy recipes for cooking with broccoli, Brussels sprouts, cabbage, cauliflower, collards, kale, kohlrabi, mustard greens, rutabaga, and turnips. Turn a bumper crop into a delicious meal. $7.95. Order #558-8.

Better Vegetable Gardens the Chinese Way. Peter Chan provides practical advice on raised-bed gardening in this attractive how-to volume. $9.95. Order #388-7.

Secrets of Plant Propagation. Lewis Hill shares his time-tested experience on how to start your own flowers, vegetables, fruits, berries, shrubs, trees, and houseplants. $12.95. Order #370-4.

These books are available at your bookstore, lawn & garden center, or may be ordered directly from Garden Way Publishing, Dept 8900, Schoolhouse Road, Pownal, VT 05261. Please add $2.50 for Fourth Class or $4.00 for U.P.S. to cover postage and handling.

References and Suggested Further Reading

Beaumont, Dr. Arthur B. *Garden Soils*. Orange Judd, New York, 1952.

Burrage, Albert C. *Burrage on Vegetables*. Van Nostrand, New York, 1954.

Cruso, Thalassa. *Making Things Grow Outdoors*. Alfred A. Knopf, New York, 1971.

Dindal, Daniel L. *Ecology of Compost*. State University of New York, 1972.

Foster, Catherine Osgood. *The Organic Gardener*. Vintage, New York, 1972.

Goldsmith, Carolyn. *Compost: A Cosmic View with Practical Suggestions*. Harper Colophon, New York, 1973.

Hunter, Beatrice Trum. *Gardening Without Poisons*. Houghton Mifflin, Boston, 1964.

Kellogg, Charles E. *Our Garden Soils*. MacMillan, New York, 1952.

Langer, Richard W. *Grow It!* Saturday Review Press, New York, 1972.

Menchofer, Larry. "A Citizen's Guide to Proper Disposal of Leaves and Other Organic Materials". Ohio Environmental Protection Agency.

Nehrling, Arno and Irene. *Easy Gardening with Drought Resistant Plants.* Hearthside, New York, 1968.

Nuese, Josephine, *The Country Garden.* Charles Scribner's Sons, New York, 1970.

Poincelot, Raymond P. "The Biochemistry and Methodology of Composting". Connecticut Agricultural Experimental Station, New Haven, 1972.

"Quick Home Compost". University of Vermont, Burlington, 1973.

Rodale, J.I. *The Organic Front.* Rodale Press, Emmaus, Penna., 1948.

Rodale, J.I. *Pay Dirt.* Devon-Adair, New York, 1948.

Rodale, J.I. *The Rodale Guide to Composting.* Rodale Press, Emmaus, Penna., 1979.

Rodale, Robert. *The Basic Book of Organic Gardening.* Rodale-Ballantine, Emmaus, Penna., 1971.

"The Science of Sanitary Odorless Composting for Homeowner or Municipality". Brookside Nurseries, Inc., Darien, Conn.

Wickenden, Leonard. *Gardening with Nature.* Fawcett, New York, 1954.

INDEX

149

potting compound, 131-133
Prescription Soil Analysis, 91
printer's ink, 63
protein, 30
putrescine, 27
psychrophiles, 16, 27-29, 98

"quicklime" (calcium oxide), 93
"Q.R. (Quick Return)", 69

rats, 33
Raymond, Dick, 124
Reader's Digest, 119
recycling, 19-20, 140, 141
rhododendrons, 58
Rodale, J.I., 16
Rodale Press, 63
rotary lawn mower, 78
rotary tiller, 103 *illus.*, 122-124,
 129, 134

sawdust, 59, 83, 94
sclerotia, 65
seaweed, 20, 59-60
shade, 36
"sheet" composting, 121-124
shells, 55-56
 clam, 56, 91
 lobster, 56
 oyster, 56, 91
shrinkage, 45
sifting, 132 *illus.*
sludge, sewage, 60-61
 "activated", 60-61
 "digested", 61
snow fence, 40
sod, 38, 41, 44, 61, 108
sodium, 60, 126
sodium nitrate *(see* fertilizer,
 chemical)
soil, 43, 44, 62, 99, 104, 108, 117
*Soil and Health: A Study of
 Organic Agriculture,* 101
South Africa, 36
spermine, 27
spores, 26, 30
Steiner, Rudolf, 16
*Step-by-Step to Organic
 Vegetable Growing,* 46, 107,
 109

stone, 41
 ground, 55-56
straw, 44, 45, 56, 60, 83, 94
Sudbury Soil Test Kit, 91-92
sulfur, 65
sun, 36, 41
Sunanda, 110
superphosphate, 64, 96
surface area, 76
synthetic fabrics, 62, 66

temperature, 17, 28-29, 41, 42, 44,
 61, 74, 82, 85, 97-100, 127
"thermal kill", 31, 61, 65, 121
thermophiles, 27-29, 61, 85
thorns, 63
"trench" composting *(see also*
 "vertical composting"),
 113-115
trace elements, 57
Troy-Bilt *(see* rotary tiller)
Truog, Emil, 131
turning, 84-87, 97, 105, 108

University of California Method,
 104-107, 125

vapor, 98
ventilation pipes, 45 *illus.*, 98, 104,
 116 illus.
vermiculite, 132
"vertical composting," 113-114,
 113-114 *illus.*
vitamins, 24, 68, 105

wart disease, 65
watering *(see* moisture)
weathering, 43, 56, 59
weeds, 20, 44, 45, 49, 61-62
weed seeds, 28, 42, 61, 85, 99,
 106, 126
weight (of compost), 45, 84
Whitman, Walt, 16
Wickenden, Leonard, 36, 40, 84
wind, 36, 37
wire mesh, 40
wood, 37, 39-40
wood chips, 76
wood preservative *(see also*
 creosote, cuprinol), 40
zinc, 60, 95, 126